OLD FRIENDS

Clive Bell was born in 1881, the son of a Welsh colliery owner and mining engineer who lived in Wiltshire. Educated at Marlborough School and King's College, Cambridge, he married Vanessa Stephen in 1906, thereby becoming brother-in-law to Virginia Woolf and a central figure within Bloomsbury.

On leaving Cambridge Bell had gone to Paris, intending to pursue historical research but in fact spending more time in the company of painters. His interest in art was further enhanced by his meeting with Roger Fry in 1910. Caught up in the excitement caused by the arrival of French Post-Impressionism in Britain, Bell's most important contribution to the ensuing debate was his book *Art*, published in 1914. In this book he demolished the existing hierarchy of aesthetic values and promoted in its place the concept of 'significant form'. He continued to write widely about modern art in the pages of the *New Statesman and Nation* and was on terms of friendship with many artists, in both England and France.

Despite various publications his output, in terms of books, did not equal his scholarly habits, for all his life he spent several hours of the day reading. In addition he was a *bon viveur*, a man whose impetuosity and generosity made him always a life-enhancing companion.

OLD FRIENDS

PERSONAL RECOLLECTIONS

Clive Bell

CASSELL · LONDON

Cassell Publishers Limited
Artillery House, Artillery Row
London SW1P 1RT

First published by Chatto & Windus: The Hogarth Press Ltd
Published in Cassell Biographies 1988

British Library Cataloguing in Publication Data

Bell, Clive, 1881–1964
    Old Friends: personal recollections.—
    (Cassell biographies).
    1. Arts—Great Britain—History—20th century
    I. Title
    709'.2'2   NX543.28

ISBN 0 304 31479 X

Cover pattern from Wiener Werkstätte reproduced by
permission of the Austrian Museum of Applied Art

Printed and bound in Great Britain by
Biddles Ltd., Guildford and Kings Lynn

CONTENTS

PREFACE
By Frances Spalding

In one of his little-known poems, privately printed in 1917, Clive Bell refers to himself as

> A loiterer in life's pleasant places,
> A well of receptivity.

In *Old Friends* this receptive loiterer introduces us to some of his friends, ponders the character of Bloomsbury and gives us a taste of artistic life in Paris at two distinct periods. Characteristic of Clive Bell is the pleasure these essays afford, for he could not enjoy any situation unless those present shared his delight. To his friend David Garnett, he seemed 'an almost perfect example of James Mill's Utilitarian theory that a man cannot become rich without enriching his neighbours'. Despite the mass of literature that has been published on Bloomsbury since these essays first appeared, they still demand to be read and re-read for the first-hand experience they contain, for the revealing anecdotes and incisive perceptions. The conversational manner which Bell adopts dispels the distancing effect of mandarin prose but it can also, now and then, seem intrusively intimate, assuming on the part of the reader familiarity with the names dropped and a too ready acceptance of the writer's values. The art critic John Russell, who was on terms of friendship with Bell, has observed that *Old Friends* is too courtly and digressive in style to convey the full flavour of its author's company. Nevertheless, until a selection of his letters is published, this is probably the book that best conveys Clive Bell's brio and attack, his crisp wit and gift for story-telling, qualities that made him an excellent conversationalist. When in January 1905 Thoby Stephen began holding 'at homes' at 46 Gordon Square, gatherings which were crucial in the formation of Bloomsbury, their success owed much to Bell's genial presence and his capacity for starting good topics of conversation.

In *Old Friends* five out of the nine essays are concerned either with Bloomsbury or certain individuals found within it. The chief purpose of the essay entitled 'Bloomsbury' is to challenge the inexact use of this term, for as early as the 1920s its meaning had degenerated, the name often being applied, very loosely, to a certain manner, slightly upper-class, witty, eccentric and undeniably intellectual. It was allocated to various individuals, among them the Sitwells, Aldous Huxley and T. S. Eliot, none of whom was a part of that intimate core to whom the label correctly belongs. This slipshod use of the term 'Bloomsbury' encouraged its detractors to constrain complex characters and their differing points of view within simplistic and often damaging straitjackets. Hence Clive Bell's indignation at the use of such phrases as 'the Bloomsbury doctrine' or 'the Bloomsbury point of view'.

It is not, however, his indignation but his sympathy that gives this book lasting value. Alert to the paradoxes and contradictions that composed Walter Sickert's character, for instance, he, better than any other, brings out the mercurial quality of this artist. His essay on Lytton is both sharp and affectionate. Strachey's 'famous irony and devastating sarcasm' are conveyed through an anecdote: listening to a *Punch* artist apologizing for the habit of lynching negroes by hinting with gentlemanlike prudery at their crime, Lytton queries: 'Yes, but are you sure the white women mind so much as all that?' Here and elsewhere Clive Bell makes us aware of the merging of sense, sensibility and morality in Bloomsbury thought and behaviour. Lytton Strachey, in particular, had unremitting standards. 'But always', Bell writes, 'there was that atmosphere, that sense of intelligent understanding mingled with affection, which induced his companion to give of his or her best in a particular way from a particular angle.'

Often Bell's perceptions of others are unflattering. We learn how irritating Maynard Keynes's cocksureness could be and how Roger Fry's open-mindedness could leave him ridiculously gullible. We might note also that Bell, despite his love of bold assertions, uses the term 'genius' warily, denying it to Sickert. Only two of his friends, he says, emanated 'simply and unmistakably' a sense of genius: one was Picasso, the other Virginia Woolf. It is therefore initially disappointing that in his essay on Woolf he expends so much energy warning us that her remarks and views could be exaggerated, unfair or even untrue. And how surprised he would be today to learn that *Three Guineas* ('her least admirable pro-duction') has been hailed by feminists as a classic, a greater achievement than *A Room of One's Own*. Nevertheless Bell's relationship with Virginia Woolf gives this essay an especial import, for it was he who first convinced her that she could write. That, wrote Bell after her death, 'seems to me the finest feather I shall ever be able to stick in my cap'.

Sheffield
1987

I

INTRODUCTION

THIS is not a collection of magazine articles, though at first sight it may look like one. Some years ago a publishing house—not Chatto and Windus—suggested tactfully, through a friend, that 'though not clean past my youth' I 'had yet some smack of age in me, some relish of the saltness of time', and that, to speak like a publisher rather than Sir John Falstaff, I had better begin to think about writing my memoirs. The word 'memoirs', with its hint of Saint-Simon and the great autobiographers, frightened me: flattered, I declined. But later it occurred to me that even I might be able to amuse a small public by giving some account of the odd and eminent people I had known; that I might reasonably attempt some modest appreciations mingled with small talk even at the risk of hearing them called memoirs. Indeed, I suppose these are memoirs of a sort. Anyhow, the proposal put an idea into my head, and I sat down to describe Walter Sickert as I knew him. That was to be the first chapter of a volume, the middle and end of which I foresaw as clearly as authors are apt to foresee such things.

I reckoned without the proverbial vanity of my trade. No sooner was the thing written than I hankered after seeing it in print. I wondered whether my friend Mr. Peter Quennell would publish it in *The*

Cornhill. He did; and I take this opportunity of thanking the present editor and the house of Murray for permission to reprint not only this but two more essays: *Lytton Strachey* and *Roger Fry*. Once again, and only once, did I betray my resolution by making an article of what should have been a chapter; and that was in my opinion a pardonable lapse. Our favourite excuse for premature publication Pope has made ridiculous for ever; yet truly it was at the request of my friend Mr. Geoffrey Hudson that I gave 'Bloomsbury' to *The Twentieth Century*. To him and to the other editors and owners of that evergreen monthly I am in debt for leave to reprint the article. It goes without saying, I hope, that this and all the other reprints have been revised and in some cases extended.

The sole contribution, perhaps I should say intrusion, which breaks the premeditated tenor of the book is the short piece on T. S. Eliot. Some admirers, on the occasion of his sixtieth birthday, thought fit to deck the poet with a florilegium. Me they invited to add a daisy or dandelion to the nosegay, and this I have included because I like to remember that Tom Eliot is an old friend. I seldom see him now, alas! But I have known him these forty years, and at one time we met pretty often. He is become a planetary figure, much sought and hardly to be found, occupied incessantly with affairs of this world and the next; so that the nearest I have come to him of late was in the London Clinic, where we were patients simultaneously and I believe on the same floor. Of whom I should ask permission to reprint this piece I do not know. To be sure, since the contribution was gratuitous, I am advised that legally no permission is required. But I am concerned less with legality than urbanity, and so I should like to say 'thank you' to somebody. The collection of tributes and memories was made by Mr. Richard March and Mr. Tambimuttu, and published by 'Editions Poetry London' in 1948. The firm apparently no longer exists; Mr. John Hayward knows not where I can find either of the editors, and what Mr. Hayward does not know about matters pertaining even remotely to literature I take to be unknowable.

Those who do me the honour of reading this book will perceive that it falls into two parts. The distinction, however, is not between the published and unpublished but between appreciations of people I knew intimately, and gossip about people whom I have known long but not very well. Of Lytton Strachey, Roger Fry, Maynard Keynes and Virginia Woolf my account, fair or unfair, is certainly based on close association, for with each I must have spent months, all told, literally under the same roof. They come first, or almost first, in the short list of people with whom I have lived on terms of perfect familiarity. We have talked about everything. We have quarrelled and made it up. With two of them, Lytton and Virginia, I carried on for thirty years and more an irregular correspondence. Of all four I could have told a hundred tales though in fact I have told only a few which seemed to illustrate the points I was trying to make. If I have misrepresented them I cannot exculpate myself on the plea of insufficient data.

With those other eminent contemporaries—Matisse, Picasso and Cocteau for instance—my relations were different. These are or were my friends, but I have not known them intimately. All I have to offer amounts to little more than tittle-tattle and random recollections; and the reader doubtless will observe that in recording these my approach is more distant, my manner less confident, than when I speak of those with whom I was familiar. To be frank, whereas I have the vanity to consider the five first chapters of this book genuine though incomplete appreciations, the two last I reckon no more than a collection of sketches and anecdotes to amuse the present generation and perhaps to instruct some future historian.

A further difference that an attentive reader will not fail to remark is a difference in the treatment of the living and the dead. 'On doit les égards aux vivants', said Voltaire, 'On ne doit aux morts que la verité'. May I add that besides 'les égards' an author writing of 'les vivants' does well to bear in mind the English law of libel?

This short introduction suffices, I hope, to explain the nature of the book to which it stands preface: there remains only the pleasant duty of thanking Mrs. Bagenal for letting me see the long, characteristic letter from Virginia Woolf, and Mr. Leonard Woolf for allowing me to print it.

Clive Bell

Charleston. August 1955

II

WALTER SICKERT

AT my preparatory school we learnt by heart a little poem called *The Chameleon*, the moral of which was, as you might guess, 'Remember others see as well as you.' Those who write or talk about Sickert would do well to bear this poem in mind; for those who knew him intimately, or at any rate saw him frequently and talked with him during thirty years or more, could never feel sure that their Sickert was Sickert's Sickert, or that Sickert's Sickert corresponded with any ultimate reality. Only the pictures were there to prove that a temperament, with an eye and a hand, called Sickert or Walter Sickert or Richard Sickert or Walter Richard Sickert existed and throughout a long development from Whistlerian days to the last could be recognised. If only the excellent Dr. Emmons had understood this, his not very good book *The Life and Opinions of Walter Richard Sickert* might have been better; but I doubt Dr. Emmons is of those who never so much as surmise that chameleons change colour. 'The opinions of Walter Richard Sickert', what were they? They boxed the compass between a first and a third glass of wine. Sickert was a chameleon, and the most I hope to suggest is some plausible explanation of the fact.

Sickert was a *poseur*: he belonged to an age of *poseurs*, the age of Wilde and Huysmans and Whistler.

If, to be an artist, it was not absolutely necessary to *épater les bourgeois*, it was necessary to do so in order to be reckoned one in the best circles. And it was in the best artistic and intellectual circles that Sickert was admired. In London, at the beginning of the century, his position was remarkable and, I think, enviable. He was not a popular artist but he was esteemed. English people of intelligence and culture, whose culture was mildly cosmopolitan and more or less up to date, had to have an English painter to admire, and whom could they have but Sickert? That he was their best may have counted for something: more to the purpose was the fact that he was neither Victorian nor precisely Edwardian, neither stodgy nor stupid nor quite respectable. Also, at that time, he was not provincial. He was a good European, a man of the great world, and well enough mannered to have taken a minor part in a novel by Henry James. He was extremely good and interesting looking: he was thoroughly presentable: and he was an actor. Never forget—Sickert never let one forget—that his earliest passion and profession was the stage.

Possibly it is significant that I met Sickert first, not in a studio, but in Bedford Square, lunching with Lady Prothero. That must have been about the year 1907; but already I had heard a great deal about him and had seen his pictures, not in London, but in Paris. I met him often during the first Fitzroy period, the period of Saturday afternoon tea-parties and discreet advertisements in *The Westminster Gazette*; and came to know him, or so it seemed, at the time of the first Post-Impressionist exhibition (1911–12). His behaviour in that affair was characteristic. Naturally the art of Cézanne, still more the art of Matisse and Picasso, was to him unsympathetic. It was, or seemed at the moment to be, a challenge to his own and to that of his masters; for in 1911, I am ashamed to say, to many of us post-impressionist meant anti-impressionist. Though Sickert never understood Cézanne, he was much too intelligent not to perceive that the Post-Impressionists were far superior to the pets of their enemies. Characteristically, he made the best, or worst, of both worlds. He jeered at Roger Fry (Rouchaud recalls having once asked him why he kept a peculiarly idiotic German picture on his mantelpiece and having received for answer 'pour emmerder Fry') and at the same time poked fun at the self-appointed defenders of orthodoxy, for instance at Mr. Henry Halliday and Sir Philip Burne-Jones. I seem to remember a letter by him in reply to one of the latter's intemperate outbursts beginning—'Let us see if Philip can be a little gentleman'. Sickert was fond of cracking jokes, some of them not bad, at my expense, which did not prevent him, when I published my first book—largely inspired by the exhibition of which he disapproved and to some extent a paean in praise of Cézanne—from publishing a long and flattering account of it in *The New Age*. Needless to say this friendly article by a friend was studded with disobliging quips. That is the sort of thing good Dr. Emmons cannot quite understand; but understood it must be if we are to get a notion of Sickert.

He was a *poseur* by choice; he was naughty by nature and he never ceased to be an actor. In order

not to be disconcerted and misled one had to know
what part at any given moment he had cast himself
for. One day he would be John Bull and the next
Voltaire; occasionally he was the Archbishop of Can-
terbury and quite often the Pope. He was an actor
in all companies and sometimes a buffoon. He would
dress up as a cook, a raffish dandy, a Seven Dials
swell, a book-maker, a solicitor, or an artist even.
And the disguise generally worked—*épaté-d* I mean:
only—so the story goes—when he went over to Paris
to see the Manet exhibition in the Orangerie dressed
up as one of the gentlemen in that master's *Musique
aux jardins des Tuileeries* did the performance fall flat.
That was a Parisian experience to which he never
referred. Also he was a rake amongst the scholars
and a scholar amongst the rakes; or rather, though
a rake he was in so far as a hardworking man who
takes his job seriously can be a rake, he was a man
of deep learning in Fitzroy Street and at Cambridge
little better than a dunce. Partly, I suppose, through
his first wife, née Cobden, he had rubbed shoulders
with what are called 'the Intellectuals', and so quick
a man had soon picked up from them a smattering
of history, politics and science. Unlike most painters
he was not wholly unfamiliar with ideas. 'Le pein-
tre', said Degas, 'en général est bête', and he might
have added 'ignorant'. Sickert would have been a
clever man in any company, clever enough to appear
to know a great deal more than he did. He had
attended lectures at King's College, and, I believe,
passed the London University matriculation examination; so we may credit him with all the erudition
these facts imply. But he was not what people in

studios and cafés believed him to be: he was not a
scholar. He was fond of quoting, and misquoting,
Latin tags in and out of season, and was not unwilling that his hearers should conclude that he was in
the habit of reading Horace with his feet on the
fender. I fancy he had dipped into a good many
books in different languages; but it was noticeable
that those which lay about in his studios remained
where they lay for months and years. French and
French slang he knew remarkably well. He could
read Goldoni's Venetian plays in the original, but I
am not sure that he ever did—all through. I dare say
he could speak German before he could read English. Certainly I remember how, one evening during
the first war, when he was dining in the Café Royal
with a lady, Sir Max Beerbohm and me, he burst
into such a torrent of German jokes and German
songs that the author of *Zuleika Dobson*—at least so
it seemed—grew slightly uneasy. It was that evening, after Sir Max had gone home, that he insisted
on showing us his 'studios'—'my drawing studio',
'my etching studio', etc. The operation involved
chartering a cab and visiting a series of small rooms
in different parts of London. These, as even in those
days there was a 'black out' of sorts, had to be visited
by match-light—the windows of course being blind-
less—and by match-light the works of art were in-
spected. Of one of them—a drawing of a woman with
long hair hanging in a plait to the waist—I happened
to say that I had known and admired the model,
whereupon Sickert insisted on my taking it, as a gift,
there and then, observing 'when a man's had a lech
on a girl he has a right to her picture'. Next day,

when we were more ourselves, I persuaded him to accept half the price he would normally have asked, and for five pounds became possessor of a little masterpiece.

Sickert was not a scholar, neither do I think he was a very good writer. Nevertheless, reading Dr. Emmon's book I discovered that his serious criticism and advice are far more interesting and better expressed than I had supposed. It would be well if these serious pieces could be collected and published in a single volume.[1] But if it is on his letters to the papers that his fame as a writer and a wit is to rest, then it will hardly survive the shock of these letters being re-read. For, to be frank, those famous letters, especially the later ones, while flaunting an air of profundity combined with scintillating snappiness, are as often as not silly, incoherent, beside the point and ungrammatical. Obviously he modelled his controversial style on Whistler's: a dangerous model, for Whistler was a born and reckless writer. As he grew older his communications to the editor of *The Times* became more incoherent and more frequent and at last suffered the crushing humiliation of being relegated to small print.

In no sense was Sickert a scholar; for, if his acquaintance with books was scrappy, his acquaintance with pictures was not much better. By his own account he used to visit the National Gallery as a boy, and as a young man we must suppose he went sometimes to the Louvre. For my part, I never met

[1]This has been done by Sir Osbert Sitwell. 'A Free House' (Macmillan, 1947).

him in either; but once I went with him to the National Gallery—for a moment, after lunch—and it was clear he did not know his way about the rooms. Almost always it is instructive to look at old masters in the company of a good painter. The only picture that seemed to hold Sickert's attention was a Canaletto, and what impressed him was the ingenious way in which the master had managed a transition from the tone of a chimney-pot to that of the circumambient atmosphere. Sickert was the last of the great Impressionists. But even in the Impressionists he took only a limited interest. He took an interest in them in so far as their art unmistakably impinged on his own. Artistically, he belonged to a small clique— a clique determined by topography rather than the bounds of the spirit. Nothing that happened within five hundred yards of Mornington Crescent or Fitzroy Square, as the case might be, was indifferent to him. A rumour that Robinson of Rathbone Place had invented a new method of rendering rime on park palings filled him with excitement not unmingled with dismay. What had been done in Florence in the fifteenth century and what was doing in Paris in the twentieth left him cold, though, in the case of Florence, deferent. He had no standards. He acquired a mass of junk from a little place round the corner and persuaded himself that it consisted mainly of paintings by Tintoretto. 'Whom else can it be by?' he would query with an impressively knowing air. Whom, indeed? always supposing that it was Venetian work of the period. For if it was not by Giorgione or Titian or Veronese only by Tintoretto could it be, since Sickert would hardly have recalled the names of other Venetian painters of the sixteenth century. But 'the work of such imaginative painters as Veronese, or, in our own time and country Leighton, Watts or Poynter . . .' (*The Times*, 3 July, 1913) may suffice to give the measure of his connoisseurship.

My admiration for Sickert's painting is, I hope, fairly well known. I have expressed it in many places at different times; and if Sickert did me the honour of treating me as a friend it was, I surmise, because he was well aware of it. I consider him the greatest British painter since Constable and almost as much above Whistler as below Degas. But I do not think he had genius; though I know that good judges hold that his extraordinarily sure sense of tone amounted to that. He had a great deal of talent, and yet perhaps less natural gift than some of his inferiors. What he had besides talent was intellect, perseverance and a grand training. For, when all insignificant niceties have been brushed aside, it is clear that Sickert acquired his technique and his discipline in the France of the 'eighties, and to find a time and place in which the art of painting was pursued and studied with at once such ardour, integrity and intelligence we must go back to the Florence of the fifteenth century. He learnt a good deal from Whistler and had the courage to forget the greater part of it; but he never forgot what he learnt from Degas. Foreign blood may have made it easier for him than it appears to be for most British painters to take his art seriously: hereditary also may have been his power of application. It was because he was both intelligent and disciplined that he never attempted to stray beyond his limits: and Sickert was limited. 'One's pictures are like one's toenails', he once said to me, 'they're one's own whether they're on or off.' I do not find the observation extraordinarily profound: it is charact-eristic in having a specious air of profundity and memorable as showing that he was at any rate will-ing to have it believed that to him his pictures were part of himself: also I doubt whether he felt as pos-sessively and affectionately about anything which was not part of himself. His art he took seriously. Not quite seriously towards the end maybe, when he took to making those comic transcripts of Victorian illustrations. That was Sickert playing the fool. And he played it so heartily and with so good a grace out-side his art that one cannot but regret he should ever have played it within. However, those facetiæ found their billets: they pleased certain ladies of fashion and amateurs who had taken to Sickert late in life; so now they hang in appropriate places, *dulce et decor-um est*, as Sickert himself might have put it, *desipere in loco*.

Anyhow, let us agree that Sickert was a great painter and completely sincere. Outside his art he was an actor, a buffoon sometimes, and a delightful companion. His buffoonery, a little trying perhaps in the funny titles he gave his pictures, became in his later public utterances distressing. That famous speech at Sadler's Wells is not a thing of which his more fastidious admirers will wish to be reminded. He liked 'showing off'. About half of what he said and wrote and nothing of what he painted—except some of those 'Echos'—was meant to startle. His feebler jokes and many of his judgments were to show how unlike he was to other men. For similar reasons he was in the habit of lighting that end of a cheroot which most people put in their mouths, and of shaving or not shaving. His extravagances and oddities, his practice of breakfasting at railway stations or of keeping a taxi ticking at one of his front doors the best part of the day, his unpaid tradesmen and overpaid waiters were all means to the same end. So, to some extent, may have been that trick of sending for a dealer and giving him a corded bale of unexamined and sometimes unfinished canvasses in return for a handful of notes. But I am far from being convinced that Sickert was a bad man of business. Like Mr. Hutton, he believed in low prices and a big turn-over. He would have argued, with elaborate and affected cynicism, that, if an artist has a studio full of pictures, it is better for him to sell fifty a year at twenty pounds apiece than two at two hundred. 'Affected', I say, because I am certain that the deep and unavowed motive was not financial. Sickert sold his pictures cheap, and gave them away too, because he liked to think of Sickerts being looked at by as many people as possible. The more Sickerts in circulation the better, he thought: and so do I.

The biographer who one day will attempt a full-length portrait of Sickert, of Sickert with all his gifts and his absurdities, his contradictions and his charm, will have to realise—I repeat and am sorry to repeat it—that Sickert was a *poseur* besides being a great painter. Also he may discover, perhaps with mild surprise, when he has to explain so many inexplicable sayings and doings and give shape to a mass of refractory data, that at bottom Sickert was a solid,

middle-class Englishman. There—he may say—
there, but for the grace of God, or the wonders of
science, went a Victorian paterfamilias. It is true
that Sickert felt most of the respectable feelings
though he generally succeeded in hiding them. When
he called Albert the good he meant it. He was gen-
uinely shocked when a married picture-dealer of his
acquaintance eloped with his secretary, and vexed
with me because I was not. 'It isn't done', he said—
I can swear to his very words: but there he was
wrong. When some young painters and students,
mainly out of a sense of inferiority I surmise, took to
pilfering in Fitzroy and Charlotte Street, he warned
the shop-keepers, and warned the young thieves that
he would tell the police; for he felt the sacredness of
the rights of property instinctively as a citizen should.
In fact, he was a sound conservative—or liberal—
and would have endorsed most of his eminent ex-
father-in-law's opinions had he been familiar with
them. One need not take very seriously his pronouncements in favour of the Fascist or Nazi systems;
so far as I know he came out with them only when
someone was about likely to rise to that bait. But it is
on printed record that he felt no pity at all for the
blameless Ethiopians and no moral indignation
against Mussolini. Sickert frequented men and
women of all kinds, not only pimps and prostitutes,
fish-wives and scavengers, but the less picturesque
classes too—shop-keepers, officers of the merchant
marine, solicitors, county-court judges and politicians. He was amused by all sorts and conditions of
men and in his way took an interest in them: but he
did not love them. If he was not a Fascist, he, like

everyone who has anything to do that requires fine thought, great skill and continuous effort, detested disorder. Yet, being an artist, he was necessarily something of an anarchist and a bit of an aristocrat: at all events, he was an anti-panisocrat, and I think he would have liked the word. Better than most he knew that all men are not equal; and I can imagine few things he would have cared for less than a classless society. Uniformity is not a dish to set before an artist: Sickert loved variety—variety in all things, in men, and women too, clothes, food, manners, ways of life. For that Καλὸς Κἀγαθός of popular philosophers, the common man, he had no respect whatever, he regarded him as a means; and, mocking our Radio Platos, he would, as likely as not, have referred them and their idol to that Authority which recommends us to learn and labour truly to get our own living and to do our duty in that state of life unto which it shall please God to call us.

III

LYTTON STRACHEY

'ANYONE can see you're a freshman, sir,' said
the head porter at the Great Gate of Trinity.
He was telling me, as tactfully as he deemed
necessary, that to carry an umbrella when wearing
a gown was contrary to custom. To soften the snub
he made a little conversation designed to show that
no one need feel the worse for a bit of advice from so
knowing a man, and, indicating another gowned
freshman who happened to be crossing the court,
observed—'You'd never think he was a general's
son.' The general's son was Lytton Strachey. Though
unbearded, already he had encouraged a weak
brown moustache, which, with his lank dark hair,
pincer eye-glasses, and long chin, added somehow
to that air of flexible endlessness which was his pre-
vailing physical characteristic. No: Lytton Strachey,
at the age of twenty, did not look a head-porter's
notion of a general's son.

Whether I made his acquaintance in Sydney-
Turner's rooms or Leonard Woolf's or Thoby
Stephen's I cannot say, only I feel sure it was within
a month of our going up. Also I think it was in our
first term that we founded the Midnight Society.
The date can be of interest only to those indefatig-
able searchers after truth who concern themselves
with the small beginnings of things; but of them one
or two may be glad to know that probably in the late

autumn of 1899 was laid the foundation of Bloomsbury. For the six members of the Midnight Society
were Saxon Sydney-Turner, Leonard Woolf, Lytton
Strachey, Thoby Stephen, A. J. Robertson and myself. Robertson, after he went down, disappeared
into the wilds of Liverpool and was never heard of
again—by me.[1] But the remaining five composed,
when they came to London, and when the band had
been reinforced and embellished by the addition of
Thoby's two sisters, Vanessa and Virginia Stephen,
the nucleus of that group to which the place of meeting—the Stephens' house in Gordon Square—was
later to give a name. But this is to anticipate by five
or six years. The Midnight Society, which met at
midnight because another—the X—of which some
of us were members, met earlier on Saturday evenings, assembled in my rooms in the New Court, and,
having strengthened itself with whisky or punch and
one of those gloomy beef-steak pies which it was the
fashion to order for Sunday lunch, proceeded to read
aloud some such trifle as *Prometheus Unbound*, *The
Cenci*, *The Return of the Druses*, *Bartholomew Fair* or
Comus. As often as not it was dawn by the time we
had done; and sometimes we would issue forth to
perambulate the courts and cloisters, halting on Hall
steps to spout passages of familiar verse, each following his fancy as memory served.

Lytton read well; and seemed to have those
squeaky notes, to which his voice rose sometimes but
by no means generally in conversation, under con-

[1] I am happy to say that, as a result of this writing, I have
heard of him again, and from him.

trol. In Restoration comedy, at unexpected but suitable moments, they would emerge, but never in high poetical drama. He was not however the best reader of the company; that honour goes to Sydney-Turner, who was also the most learned of the set. Leonard Woolf was the most passionate and poetical; Lytton the most grown-up; Thoby Stephen and I were deemed worldly because we smoked cigars and talked about hunting. Lytton, however, liked us the better for that.

What with sitting for a fellowship, which, by the way, he never obtained, what with one thing and another, Lytton must have lived in Cambridge, on and off, the best part of ten years. I was up for four, and a good part of my last year was spent in London. Thus it comes about that when I tell stories of Lytton at Cambridge men a little junior to me look amazed and incredulous. They think they knew him well, and so they did; only it was in the second—the King's period—that they knew him. In the years after I went down—after 1903, that is to say—Lytton when he was at Cambridge, more or less lived in King's; so much so, that when, at the time of the second Post-Impressionist Exhibition (1912), a University paper published a reproduction of Henry Lamb's portrait (not the big portrait in the Tate, but a head) and below it printed 'Lytton Strachey (King's)' few seemed aware of the error. In this second period two Kingsmen, Sheppard and Keynes, were, I suppose, his closest friends, though Norton of Trinity may have been almost as intimate: students will recall that *Eminent Victorians* is dedicated to H. T. J. N. But in my time his friends were mostly in his own college: there were, beside his cronies of the Midnight Society, McLaren (the mathematician), Hawtrey and George Trevelyan (a young and ardent don, violently radical, already marked out as a future Master); and of an older generation Verrall, Duff, MacTaggart. Also, of course, there was G. E. Moore, the philosopher, who at that time, and, as some maintain, ever after, was the dominant influence in all our lives. From London, with commendable regularity and a faint air of mystery, would come on Saturdays Bertrand Russell, E. M. Forster and Desmond MacCarthy: these also were friends, and I suspect they were the death of the Midnight.

The influence of Lytton while I was at Cambridge was appreciable but not great; it was after I had gone down that it became so impressive as to leave a mark on at least three generations of undergraduates. In my time it was mainly literary. As I have said, Lytton, who had not suffered the disadvantage of a public school education, was more grown-up than the rest of us—it should be remembered that in the Midnight Society were no Etonians—and his literary taste was more adult. To be sure, he had read less English—to say nothing of Latin and Greek of which, I surmise, he knew about as much as Shakespeare—than Turner or Woolf; but amongst newly fledged undergraduates, late sixth-form boys, he seemed to stand for culture or something like it. He had read a little French. He had admired Joachim. He had attended private views, and doted on Melville. He and I were, I believe, singular in our set, if not in the University, in that we took some interest in the visual arts. I am still surprised, and disconcerted maybe, on going into a modern don's rooms to find there a nice collection of contemporary paintings. It is so unlike the dear old days when an Arundel print or two represented the *ne plus ultra* of academic æstheticism. But Lytton and I, while still in *statu pupillari* if you please, once met by chance in the National Gallery and more than once in the Fitzwilliam. There he would bid me admire Veronese's *Semele* which he admired inordinately—for literary reasons—and about the authenticity of which I now have the gravest doubts. Also one of my earliest excursions in æsthetics must have been provoked by his query, as he contemplated the reproduction of a Degas pinned to my door—'I wonder what the uninitiated really think about it'.

Certainly Lytton helped to stimulate that enthusiasm for the lesser Elizabethans, and for Sir Thomas Browne, which came to boiling point about the time I was leaving Cambridge; and when at the beginning of our second year he developed a slightly affected passion for Pope he took us by surprise but he took us with him. He was a great figure, and in a world of very young men a great figure is, I suppose, bound to be a considerable influence. In public, at meetings of clubs and societies that is to say, and at Dons' evenings, his appearances were impressive and his comments noted. I recall a meeting of the Sunday Essay Society at which Bray—one, and the most sympathetic, of the Christian intellectuals and a judge's son to boot—anxious to be fair and reasonable in a teleological argument, put it to Lytton—'I expect, Strachey, you would maintain that self-realisation was the end of existence'. To which Strachey replied: 'My dear Bray, that would certainly be the *end*'. That struck us as worthy of Voltaire. And it is perhaps significant that when I had the good fortune to meet in my first year Desmond MacCarthy, travelling by train from King's Cross to Cambridge, and persuade him to lunch with me next day, it was Lytton whom I at once invited as the most suitable of my friends to entertain this charming and distinguished stranger. Of course it turned out they had already met.

But mainly Lytton's influence was literary; and in those early days it could hardly have been anything else. Philosophically we were dominated by Moore, and politics we despised. Let politicians disport themselves at the Union, where such small fry looked big; we lik.d some of them well enough in a patronising way. Nevertheless, the outside world— by which I mean the University—must have been dimly aware of Lytton's existence, must have heard something of him and disliked what it heard, for *The Granta* devoted one of a series of humorous pieces entitled *People I have not met* to 'the Strache'—the interviewer discovering him, robed in an embroidered silk dressing-gown, reclining on a sofa, smoking scented cigarettes and sipping *crème de menthe*. The Strache, if I remember rightly, was made to close the colloquy with the cryptic utterance—'Oh virtue, virtue, life is a squiggle,' from which it would appear that his reputation was not purely literary after all. Readers of *The Granta*, I dare say, called him a 'decadent'.

Be that as it may, it was not till after I had left Cambridge and Paris and returned to London that

I realised Lytton's influence was beginning to touch life at various points and at points not far from the centre. I have a few letters from this first period; mostly they are dated, and they could be placed were they not. All begin 'Dear Bell' or 'My dear Bell'; the first beginning 'Dear Clive' is of November 25th, 1906. This is a date in the history of Bloomsbury. It was at the time of my engagement to Vanessa Stephen that we took to Christian names, and it was entirely Lytton's doing. No question here of drifting into a habit, the proposal was made formally when he came to congratulate us. The practice became general; and though perhaps it marked a change less significant than that symbolised by the introduction of the Greek dual, it has had its effect. Henceforth between friends manners were to depend on feelings rather than conventions.

I have set down in some detail these salient memories because I was one of Lytton's early friends. Friends we remained—I might say cronies—friends close enough to quarrel and make it up, but the sayings and doings of later life, when Lytton had become a public character, are matter for a biographer rather than a memorialist. Nevertheless, having recorded these *juvenilia*, I should like to say a word, or rather my word, about the writer whom I admired, but also knew intimately, and of whose art and scope I am perhaps as good a judge as another. His attitude to life was informed by that genius for good sense which is apt to express itself in what sounds like paradox to the general; and Lytton's good sense came sometimes as a shock to the early twentieth century much as Wilde's came to the 'eighties' and early 'nineties'. I remember his petrifying a party of Highland sportsmen by replying to a *Punch* artist, who, after pompously deprecating the habit of lynching negroes, had added, 'but you know what it is they lynch them for'.—'Yes, but are you sure the white women mind as much as all that?' An apology for lynching made with an air of gentlemanlike prudery, was the sort of thing that made Lytton angry. For he could be angry though he rarely lost his temper. Against the popular conception of him as a sublimely detached person sitting stroking his beard, godlike and unmoved, contemplating the fussy activities of this disintegrating ant-hill which men call Earth, I have nothing to say except that it is not true. To me it is sympathetic: it is rational; it is pretty; but it is not true. They likened him to Gibbon and Voltaire, his style owes something to both—but only from the Frenchman was he directly descended. That famous irony and that devastating sarcasm were not the fruits of an immense indifference coupled with a mild Gibbonian surprise, but sprang, like Voltaire's, from indignation. It was not because he thought of them as insects that he made so many eminent Victorians look small; but because in his heart he could not help comparing them with full-sized human beings. Lytton Strachey was no more indifferent and passionless than Voltaire himself. He might have taken *Écrasez l'infâme* for his motto: I am not sure that he did not.

Like all moralists he had his standards, unlike most he kept his temper and was never self-righteous. His standards came of no wretched personal fads or conventional prejudices but were based on an acute sense of the past. It is this sense which conditions his attitude to the Victorians: for to him the Oxford of Newman and the London of Mr. Gladstone were not more real than the Paris of the Encyclopædists nor as sympathetic as the Athens of Pericles. And if you believe in the continuous identity of the race, if you believe that the human heart and brain have not contracted nor the glands dried up, if you believe that the Athenians in their passionate search for truth and their endeavour to realise their ideal were using faculties similar to those bestowed on liberals and conservatives, and if you have admired the broad grin of fatuity conferred by the scientific century on itself, why then you will have a subject for high and bitter comedy, out of which, if you happen to be Lytton Strachey, you may create a work of manifest beauty and implicit admonition.

It is legitimate to regard this humorous and witty historian, who contrives to enlighten without for a moment boring, as the descendant of Voltaire, provided you do not forget that he is at nearest great-great-grandson. Between them lie those discoveries of psychology which made it impossible for Lytton Strachey to treat life with the intellectual confidence of his ancestor. Life, he knew, was something of which the dimmest comprehension—to say nothing of the least amelioration—is more difficult than to the mind of the eighteenth century appeared its complete explanation and perfection. Overlook the fact that he defended Rousseau on the ground that Rousseau was 'a modern man', and as such incomprehensible to his contemporaries, and you mistake inevitably his point of view. The idea that he was insensitive to that side of life for which Rousseau suffered seems fantastic to anyone who knew him well; and the notion that he misjudged the Victorian age, as the revenant he is sometimes supposed to have been must have misjudged it, is absurd. In his criticism of men, of their conduct and motives, there is no failure to appreciate or sympathise with their modernity; and the 'age of progress', with all its good and bad luck, is weighed fairly in the balance and found, by comparison with the greatest—silly.

So it is a mistake to call Lytton Strachey '*dix-huitième*'. He belongs to no particular school: all one can say is, he was of the great tradition, which does not mean that he was old-fashioned or reactionary. The tradition (as you may have heard) is a live thing, growing always, growing and spreading like a tree; and the ape who would creep back to the trunk is as surely lost as the fool who would detach himself from the twig. Lytton was not at odds with his age; if he could see that there was much to be said for the Whig oligarchy and the system it maintained, he could see that there was much to be said for Socialism too. In art or life or politics always it is silly to be crying for last month's moon, and even sillier to cut loose from the tradition and play at being Adam and Eve. Lytton was a good deal less silly than most of us. His attitude to life, and therefore his art, was based on a critical appreciation of the past, an interest in the present, and a sense of human possibilities —the amalgam bound together and tempered by a fine pervasive scepticism. He judged men and their doings, as he judged books, out of knowledge, sympathy and doubt; and because he understood what human beings had achieved he was not indifferent to their fate.

Having said so much of Lytton's attitude to life, I should like to say a word about the manner in which he expressed it. Naturally not in the manner in which Voltaire did justice to *le grand siècle*, nor that in which Gibbon unrolled the doom of the Roman empire, did this modern tell his tale. His style, though like most good styles it acknowledges its ancestry, is as personal as that of any well educated author of his time. To hear some critics talk you might suppose it was precious; whereas, in fact, Lytton was rather careless about words. Yet minute attention to words is, I take it, the essence of preciosity. In the prose of an author whose acute sense of words induces a tendency to this defect or ornament —I know not which to call it—you will generally find a concatenation of half-buried metaphors which often escapes the notice of casual readers. You will find words conditioning words by recondite influences: the artist having been so intensely aware of their precise and original meanings that he has felt bound to relate each to some other which recognises the original meaning and honours the implicit association. Thus do the sentences of the more elaborate stylists tend to become a series of almost imperceptible cognate relations; and these relations, forced on the attention of the insensitive, tend to annoy. Let me give a glaring example: 'If anyone were so sanguine, a glance at the faces of our Conscript Fathers along the benches would soon bleed him'. Lytton Strachey would hardly have written that, though it is not to be supposed that he was less aware than Sir Max Beerbohm of the meaning of the word 'sanguine'. Similarly, anyone as sharply and incessantly conscious of the exact and original meaning of words as Sir Max would be unlikely to speak of 'this singular opinion' when he meant this unusual and slightly ludicrous one: but Lytton does, and so, for that matter, does Gibbon.

Writing in sentences rather than words, and in paragraphs rather than sentences, Lytton comes nearer to Macaulay than to Gibbon, and is, I should say, freer, though more elaborate, than Macaulay. The paragraph is his pattern, and he a mosaicist on the grand scale, willing, I mean, to compose out of the oddest bits. To the intrinsic quality of the cube he is indifferent almost, provided it does its work: ready-made phrases, exclamatory interjections, dramatic aposiopesis and frank journalese serve his turn: and so masterly is his art that he makes all tell, a lump of broken bottle here foiling there a die of purest *lapis*. He is a master but a dangerous one to learn of. No precious author and very few careful stylists would write: 'The light thrown by the Bible upon the whole matter seemed somewhat dubious' —'the influential circles of society'—'an excellent judge of horse-flesh'. In full dress Gibbon would never have written: 'Ward forced him forward step by step towards—no! he could not bear it;' nor I think would Macaulay. But Dr. Johnson himself might have observed with pleasure that, 'Dyspeptic by constitution, melancholic by temperament, he could yet be lively on occasions, and was known as a wit in Coburg'. For my part, I would change nothing in Lytton's style; the stock phrase and the costumier's adjective used for purposes of irony and sarcasm become delicate weapons in the hand of a master: only I would observe that they are much too treacherous to be played with by girls and boys.

I have tried to indicate in a few paragraphs—and the attempt was impertinent no doubt—what was Lytton's attitude to life and how he chose to express it. To describe the effect of this attitude on the age in which he flourished will be the task of some historian, and him I would gladly help out with a few anecdotes illustrating Lytton's reforms in the matter of free speech could I recall any that were at once significant and printable. The business ought not to be too risky seeing that what seemed downright smut to Edwardian gentility sounds conversational enough today. But either my memory or my courage fails me. Oblivion will not be cheated by my indiscreet revelations; and, anyhow, it was through his writings that Lytton's influence was spread widely, though perhaps a trifle thin. It was felt most deeply by his friends of course, and by them maybe was most effectively disseminated. With them he created a peculiar atmosphere—an atmosphere conditioned naturally by the person he happened to be with. He was extraordinarily sympathetic and provoked confidences. Gradually he must have come to know his friends' secret thoughts about most things, including themselves. Yet there was seldom anything tense in a conversation with Lytton; it drifted hither and thither in that pleasant atmosphere, gay, truthful (cynical if you will—the terms are interchangeable almost), amusingly and amusedly censorious. Lytton brought a literary and historical flavour into his talk so that, if the past were discussed sometimes as though it were the present, the perplexities and misfortunes of his contemporaries were treated often as though they came from the pages of Saint-Simon or Horace Walpole. But always there was that atmosphere, that sense of intelligent understanding mingled with affection, which induced his companion to give of his or her best in a particular way from a particular angle. I should despair of resurrecting the ghost of an idea of what I have in memory were it not that a lady, speaking of him soon after his death, let fall a melancholy but illuminating remark which seems to me to suggest the quality of his company, 'Don't you feel', said she, 'there are things one would like to say and never will say now?' And by this she did not mean affectionate things, flattering things, things that would have shown Lytton what one felt for him or thought of him, but mere comments on life or books or art or acquaintances or historical characters, little jokes and little ironies, paradoxes that were almost true and truisms masquerading as inventions, things to which the climate would have given a peculiar relish, things that now will never come to life.

Of this peculiar quality is any taste to be found and enjoyed in his writing? Yes, I think so. Sometimes when, with demurest deference, he exposes the outrageous follies of mankind as though he were recording the fruits of profound cogitation and ripe political wisdom—as indeed he often is—one catches an echo of his voice. And sometimes, when he indulges a turn for that subtle kind of fun which is the extension into the universal of a private joke, one fancies oneself back at Tidmarsh. The family joke, coterie humour, we know: in every school and college, in every clique and set, are sources of merriment which for the outside world do not exist. But there are writers—and in this English writers are perhaps especially happy—who can make a coterie of all the world. The esoteric joke depends, not only on common experience but on common assumptions; and there are writers—Sterne, Charles Lamb, Byron, Peacock—who persuade us, apparently without trying, to accept theirs and divine them even. Though we have been told very little about their favourite butts, we laugh at them mercilessly because we laugh with the marksman. And already are we so much in Lytton's humour that when, on the fourth page of his essay, he remarks of Dr. Arnold that 'his legs, perhaps, were shorter than they should have been', we know that it is all up with the headmaster of Rugby.

Unless he was feeling ill, as too often he was, Lytton with his intimate friends, or with people to whom he had taken a fancy, was delightful; but his company manners could be bad. I do not know whether it was vanity or some more recondite motive that made him unwilling to speak, or give any sign of taking an interest in the conversation, when he could not be sure of appearing as he wished to appear. Once or twice he has been with me in France, and once or twice in my flat in the company of French or French-speaking people and on such occasions he could be downright grumpy. Yet he spoke French no worse than many I have heard disporting themselves cheerfully in that language: possibly his skin was thinner than theirs. Be that as it may, in practical matters—and a party is a practical matter—Lytton was not helpful. He was something self-conscious and he was not generous. I do not mean that he was stingy, though, having been till near the end of his life rather hard up, he was always careful of his money; I mean that he was sparing of praise, a trifle envious maybe, and disinclined to put himself out for or make himself useful to others. Assuredly, he was not inconsiderate, but I suppose he was rather selfish and a thought arrogant. He took care of number one, as my old nurse used to say, and I do not blame him.

Lytton could love, and perhaps he could hate. To anyone who knew him well it is obvious that love and lust and that mysterious mixture of the two which is the heart's desire played in his life parts of which a biographer who fails to take account will make himself ridiculous. But I am not a biographer; nor can, nor should, a biography of Lytton Stachey be attempted for many years to come. It cannot be attempted till his letters have been published or at any rate made accessible, and his letters should not be published till those he cared for and those who thought he cared for them are dead. Most of his papers luckily are in safe and scholarly hands. The habit of cashing in on a man's reputation while it is still warm grows apace, and—but, to avail myself of Strachean aposiopoesis, it is time to make an end.

It was towards the end of November that I came back from Venice in 1931. A day or two after my return Lytton dined with me. He was feeling ill and went away early saying, 'let us meet again very soon when I am better'. So we dined together on the following Friday and enjoyed one of those evenings which Lytton contrived to turn into works of art. Next day I went into Wiltshire, and at Paddington discovered that Lytton, with his sister Philippa and some other relations I think, was travelling in the same coach. He came to see me in my compartment, where I was alone, and we had some talk, mostly I remember about my tussle with the Commissioners of Inland Revenue, who, as usual, were behaving disagreeably. At Reading he rejoined his party. At Hungerford I watched him walk along the platform on his way out. That was the last time I saw Lytton.

IV

MAYNARD KEYNES

IN a memoir called 'My Early Beliefs' Lord Keynes, describing the company he kept at Cambridge, finds a word or phrase to fit each of his friends: 'Moore himself was a puritan and a precisian', he writes, 'Strachey (for that was his name at that time) a Voltairean, Woolf a rabbi, myself a nonconformist, Sheppard a conformist and (as it now turns out) an ecclesiastic, Clive a gay and amiable dog, Sydney-Turner a quietist, Hawtrey a dogmatist and so on'. Now Clive may have been gay and amiable and a dog, but Maynard can have known it only by hearsay; for, oddly enough, at Cambridge we never met. Or did we meet for a moment, before dinner, before a debate? I think not; though I distinctly remember Edwin Montagu telling me that he had invited a brilliant freshman, just up from Eton, who would be of great value—when we had gone down—to the Liberal Party in the Union.[1] That was in the late autumn of 1902, and that was the first I heard of Maynard. That we did not know each other may be accounted for perhaps by the fact that I spent a good part of my last, my fourth, year (October 1902–3) in London working at the Record Office, and when I was in Cambridge lived mostly

[1]In my last year I seem to have grown out of my early contempt for politics.

with my old friends in Trinity, not accompanying
Lytton Strachey on his excursions into King's. Be
that as it may, certain I am that the first time I met
Maynard to talk to was in the summer of 1906, when
Lytton brought him to my chambers in the Temple.
He was then, I surmise, sitting for the civil service
examination, and wearing, I am sure, a light green
Burberry and a bowler hat.[1]

Our acquaintance must have improved steadily.
In February 1908 my elder son was born; and, as in
those days it was customary for a young mother to
remain in bed for perhaps a month after giving birth
to a child, I took to inviting some agreeable friend
who after dinner would entertain the convalescent
with an hour's conversation. Maynard was one of
the three or four who came. Nevertheless we cannot
yet have been what I should call intimate since I
remember feeling, not exactly shy, but conscious of
the fact that this was the first time I had dined with
him en tête-à-tête. He was still a clerk in the India
Office, living in one of those dreary blocks of flats
near St. James's Park Station; but a few months
later he returned to Cambridge, and though during
the next year or two I saw him much in company I

---

[1] May I, while correcting one mistake, irrelevantly call attention to another? On page 79 of 'Two Memoirs' Maynard
writes—'Many years later he (D. H. Lawrence) recorded in a
letter which is printed in his published correspondence, that I
was the only member of Bloomsbury who had supported him
by subscribing for Lady Chatterley.' This, if I am to be reckoned a member of Bloomsbury, is, like so many things that
Lawrence said, untrue. My subscription copy, duly numbered
578 and signed, stands now in my book-case.

rarely saw him alone. He stayed with us in the country; he was with us at Guildford in July 1911 and he it was who, having as usual secured first look at *The Times*, told us that the Lords had passed the Parliament Act: when he took Asheham for the Easter holidays my wife and I stayed with him. Evidently in August 1913 we were on easy and amiable terms for we shared a tent on a camping-party, organised by the Olliviers of course—the Brandon Camp: I recall most vividly the discomfort. Maynard minded less, he was a better camper-out than I. On the other hand he was an even worse lawn-tennis player. We played occasionally on the hilly courts of Gordon Square—he and I, Gerald Shove, Phillip Morrell and sometimes Adrian Stephen. But Maynard was so feeble that though we always gave him for partner, Phillip, by far the best of the bunch, we could not make a game of it. Maynard was dropped.

This must have been just before the first war, in the summer of 1914, when Maynard was lodging in Brunswick Square. During the winter he had served on a Royal Commission on Indian currency and consequently had begun to make friends in high places. A new Maynard, who accompanied but never displaced the old, was emerging—a man of great affairs and a friend of the great. Also, I fancy, it was about this time or a little earlier that he took to speculating. According to an account he once gave me— in whimsical mood I must confess—Maynard, who at Cambridge and in early London days had barely glanced at 'Stock Exchange Dealings', grew so weary —this is what he told me—of reading the cricket-scores in *The Times* that, while drinking his morning tea, he took to studying prices instead. You may believe it or not as you choose: anyhow it was a digression from what I was saying, that already before the war Maynard had come into contact with a part of the political and high official world. Some of us shook our heads, not over the new interests but over the new friendships. Would they not encourage the growth of what we were pleased to consider false values? Would he not soon be attaching more importance to means (power, honours, conventions, money) than to ends—i.e. good states of mind (*vide Principia Ethica passim*)? Would he not lose his sense of proportion? But when Maynard, having invited to dinner two of his big-wigs (Austen Chamberlain and McKenna I seem to remember), discovered at the last moment that all his Champagne had been drunk by Duncan Grant and his boon companions— Duncan's mid-day Champagne-parties in Brunswick Square were a feature of that memorable summer— he took it well enough. His sense of values appeared to be intact. And I will not doubt he realised that a subsequent party to which he and Duncan Grant invited the St. John Hutchinsons—Mrs. Hutchinson was Duncan's cousin—Molly MacCarthy ánd myself was much greater fun.

In September 1914 Maynard was with us at Asheham; and it pleases me to remember that the great man—and he was a great man—who enjoyed for years an international reputation for cool and detached judgment, rebuked me sharply for refusing to believe in the Russian-troops-in-England fairy tale and for surmising that the war would not soon be over. The fact is, of course, that Maynard's judgment would have been as sound as his intellect was powerful had it really been detached; but Maynard was an incorrigible optimist. I am not likely to forget the infectious confidence with which he asserted in 1929 that the Liberals were bound to have more than a hundred seats in the new House of Commons and would probably have a hundred and fifty (in fact they had 59); for he backed his opinion by a gamble on the Stock Exchange in which he involved some of his impecunious friends—I was not one of them. With considerateness as characteristic as his confidence, when he realised the awkwardness of the scrape into which his optimism had led them, he shouldered their liabilities. In 1939, towards the middle of July, when he was about to leave for a cure at Royat, he asked me whether I thought war would break out that autumn or whether there would be 'another hullabaloo'. ('Hullabaloo' seems to me quite a good name for Munich). I said that, having committed ourselves, foolishly in my opinion, to defend Poland, and Hitler being obviously determined to invade Poland forthwith, I supposed war before winter was inevitable. This time Maynard did not exactly rebuke me, but he did call me a 'pessimist'.

During the 1914–18 war I saw a good deal of him, especially during the later part, when he and I, Sheppard and Norton, shared 46 Gordon Square. It seems not generally to be known—though Mr. Roy Harrod has not attempted to conceal the fact—that Lord Keynes was a conscientious objector. To be sure he was an objector of a peculiar and, as I think, most reasonable kind. He was not a pacificist; he did not object to fighting in any circumstances;

he objected to being made to fight. Good liberal that he was, he objected to conscription. He would not fight because Lloyd-George, Horatio Bottomley and Lord Northcliffe told him to. He held that it was for the individual to decide whether the question at issue was worth killing and dying for; and surely he was entitled to consider himself a better judge than the newspaper-men who at that time ruled the country. He was surprised and shocked when Mr. Asquith gave way to their clamour. His work at the Treasury, which by 1917 had become of vital importance, kept him in contact with the more important ministers, and he saw right through Lloyd-George. He detested his demagogy. I remember his cutting from a French paper—*Excelsior* presumably—a photograph of 'the goat' as he always called him, in full evening dress and smothered in ribbons, speaking at a banquet in Paris; and I remember his writing under it 'Lying in state'. He pinned it up in the dining-room at forty-six. Later, in the supposed interests of the Liberal Party, he collaborated with 'the goat' who had become for certain left-wing papers and politicians a sort of 'grand old man'. No good came of that. As for his conscientious objection, he was duly summoned to a tribunal and sent word that he was much too busy to attend.

There are those who maintain that Maynard's importance during the war and familiarity with the great bred that cocksureness which was his most irritating characteristic. I do not agree. The influence of the great on Maynard was slight compared with Maynard's influence on them. The cocksureness was always there; circumstances evoked and possibly stimulated it. Certainly the habit was provoking. It was also amusing. Late one night towards the end of the first war I remember his coming up to my room in Gordon Square where Norton and I were talking quietly about, as likely as not, the meaning of meaning. He was elated; he had been dining; what is more, he had been dining with cabinet ministers. The question had arisen—'Who finally defeated Hannibal?' No one knew except Maynard and he told them it was Fabius Maximus: 'unus homo nobis cunctando restituit rem' he declaimed, and I hope he translated it for the politicians though for us he was good enough to leave it in the original. Of course it was not the cunctator but Scipio Africanus who finally defeated Hannibal at the battle of Zama, as I obligingly pointed out. Maynard disregarded my correction in a way that did perhaps ever so slightly suggest that someone who had been dining with cabinet ministers knew better, and continued to expatiate on the pleasures of the evening, his little historical triumph, the excellent cooking and above all the wine.

Maynard laid down the law on all subjects. I dare say I minded too much: many of his friends took it as a joke. But I do think it was silly of him; for by dogmatising on subjects about which he knew nothing he sometimes made himself ridiculous to those who did not know him well and to those who did annoying. Cocksureness was his besetting sin, if sin it can be called. Gradually it became his habit to speak with authority: a bad habit which leads its addicts to assume that the rest of us are ready to assume that their knowledge must be greater than ours. Maynard knew a good deal about a great many things, and on several subjects spoke with warranted authority. Unfortunately he got into the habit of speaking with authority whether it was warranted or not. He acquired—I do not say he cultivated—a masterful manner; and when he spoke of matters about which he knew little or nothing with the confidence and disregard for other people's opinions which were perhaps excusable when he was talking about economics or probability of rare editions, instead of appearing masterly he appeared pretentious. That, too, was a pity, for he was not pretentious; he made no boast of his superior knowledge and expected no praise for it, he merely assumed it. For my part, I was exasperated most often by his laying down the law on painting and painters; but I will not draw an example of his misplaced self-confidence from his pronouncements on art, because, æsthetic judgments being always questionable, though I am sure that his were often wrong, I am far from sure that mine are always right. Instead, I will recall a conversation—or should I say an exposition?—which remains extremely clear in my memory, and provides an instance of misplaced self-confidence the misplacedness of which is not open to dispute.

He had been staying with one of his rich city-friends—for in those days (the early 'twenties') there were still rich men in England: he had been staying in Hampshire I think but I am not sure, certainly in the south, and he returned to Charleston, the house in Sussex which for a while he shared with my wife, myself and Duncan Grant, and told us all about it. It had been a shooting party; Maynard himself never handled a gun, but he told us all about it. He told us what is done and what is not done; he told us when you might shoot and when you might not shoot, he told us how to shoot and what to shoot. And as he was under the impression—all this happened long before he had a farm and a wood of his own—that his party had been shooting grouse in Hampshire or thereabouts with rifles, you can imagine the sort of nonsense he made of it. Now it so happens I was brought up in a sporting family: I have possessed a game-licence since I was sixteen and walked with the guns since I was a child; and I do believe I have killed every game-bird in the British Isles except a capercailzie and some of the rarer duck. But if you suppose that these facts would have daunted Lord Keynes, all I can say is—you have got the great economist wrong.

My insistence on Maynard's cocksureness may have given the impression that he was spoilt by success. If so, I have given a false impression. Maynard floated happily on a sea of power and glory and considerable wealth, but never went out with the tide. Two stout anchors held him fast to shore: his old friends and Cambridge. This Mr. Roy Harrod has made clear in his excellent biography. Cabinet Ministers and *The Times* might praise, but if he had an uneasy suspicion that Lytton Strachey, Duncan Grant, Virginia Woolf and Vanessa Bell did not share their enthusiasm, public flattery might appear something to be ashamed of. When he came to Charleston with Lady Keynes for the first time after his peerage had been announced he was downright sheepish. 'We have come to be laughed at' he said.

And what was Cambridge thinkng? Maynard cared
passionately for his country, but I believe he was at
greater pains to improve the finances of King's than
to rescue those of the British Empire. If this be a
slight exaggeration, that artistic temperament, from
which I should like to be supposed to suffer, must
bear the blame; but that stern, unbending economist, Mr. Roy Harrod, has made it clear to all who
read that Keynes valued the good opinion of his old
friends far above that of the majority or the great.
Mr. Harrod, it seems to me, gives an excellent
account of his subject—I had almost said his 'hero'
—which should be read for its own sake and perhaps
as a corrective to mine. Nevertheless I understand
the feelings of those old and intimate friends who say
—'Maynard was not really like that, he was not like
that at all'. That is what old friends will always say
of official biographies; and they will be right. Mrs.
Thrale, who knew Johnson far longer and far more
intimately than Boswell knew him, doubtless said as
much. And of course Mrs. Thrale was right. Only
she forgot that it was Boswell's business to write a
biography, to depict a man in all his activities and
in his relations to all sorts of people, while it was her
privilege to record a personal impression.

I, too, am recording a personal impression. I am
trying to remember little things that have escaped
the notice of my betters. Such things are trivial by
definition, and sometimes derogatory; but, though
they may be beneath the dignity of history, they
matter a good deal in daily life. My recollections, I
foresee, run the risk of appearing spiteful. To count-
eract this appearance I could of course pile up well

merited compliments. But of what use would it be for me to expatiate on the power of Maynard's intellect and his services to humanity when writers far better qualified have done it already and done it with authority? Nevertheless, to escape the charge of malignity, let me say here and now what maybe I shall have occasion to repeat. Maynard was the cleverest man I ever met: also his cleverness was of a kind, gay and whimsical and civilized, which made his conversation a joy to every intelligent person who knew him. In addition he had been blest with a deeply affectionate nature. I once heard him say, humorously but I believe truly, at dinner, before a meeting of the memoir club, 'If everyone at this table, except myself, were to die tonight, I do not think I should care to go on living'. He loved and he was beloved. He did not love, though he may have rather liked, me; and I did not love him. That should be borne in mind by anyone who does this sketch the honour of a reading.

In great things he was magnificently generous; generous to his country, generous to his college, generous to servants and dependents, particularly generous to his less fortunate friends (I know two charming young men who may or may not know that they were educated—and highly educated—partly at his expense). In small things, however, like many who have enjoyed the advantages and disadvantages of a serious, non-conformist upbringing, he was careful. Also, financier that he was, he loved a bargain. One summer's evening in 1919 he returned to Charleston from a day in London bearing a heavy parcel which contained innumerable minute tins of potted meat.

He had bought them at a sale of surplus army-stores and he had bought them at a penny a piece. The private soldiers had not liked the stuff, and therein had shown good taste. I teased Maynard by pretending that the meat had been condemned as unfit for human consumption: and indeed, the bargain-hunter himself could barely keep it down. But at a penny a tin. . . . Again, I remember being with him at Lewes races, and asking a farmer of my acquaintance for 'a good thing'. Maynard did not want 'a good thing'; what he wanted was the best bet. He wanted a bargain in odds. This rather complicated notion puzzled my friend, and we left him puzzling. For I did not attempt to explain that what Maynard had in mind was that there might be some horse in some race against which the odds were longer than need be, or rather, book-makers being what they are, less short than might have been expected. If there were a starter at a hundred to one which might just as well have been offered at sixty-six to one, that horse, though standing no apparent chance of winning, was the horse for Maynard's money. What he wanted was not a winner but a bargain.

Lytton Strachey used to say—'Pozzo has no æsthetic sense'.[1] That was an exaggeration perhaps.

[1] Mr. Roy Harrod writes in a note: 'For many years in Bloomsbury Keynes was familiarly known by the name of Pozzo, having been so christened by Strachey after the Corsican diplomat, Pozzo di Borgo—not a diplomat of evil motive or base conduct, but certainly a schemer and man of many facets'. But it was not only, nor chiefly, of the Corsican diplomat that Lytton and those who used the nickname were thinking. The Italian word 'pozzo' has more than one meaning, and to English ears carries various suggestions.

What may be said confidently is that he had no innate feeling for the visual arts. Had he never met Duncan Grant he would never have taken much interest in painting. He made a valuable collection because generally he bought on good advice; when he relied on his own judgment the result was sometimes lamentable. Lamentable it would have been had he relied on his own judgment to the end when he wrote that piece in *The New Statesman* about Low's drawings; for in the original version, not only had he compared Low with Daumier, he had likened him to Daumier, had almost equalled him with Daumier. What he insisted on retaining is sufficiently tell-tale.

'We all know that we have amongst us today a cartoonist in the grand tradition. But, as the recognition, which contributions to evening papers receive by word of mouth round the dinner-table, cannot reach the modest cartoonist, one welcomes a book like this as an opportunity to tell Low how much we think of him and how much we love him. He has the rare combination of gifts which is necessary for his craft—a shrewd and penetrating intelligence, wit, taste, unruffled urbanity, an indignant but open and understanding heart, a swift power of minute observation with an equally swift power of essential simplification, and, above all, a sense and talent for beauty, which extracts something delightful even out of ugliness. One may seem to be piling it on, but Low really has these things, and it is a great addition to our lives to meet the tongue and eye of a civilized man and true artist when we open the *Evening Standard*.

Last summer Low and Kingsley Martin made a trip to Bolshieland, and this agreeable book is the outcome. Low's pencil and charcoal sketches are reproduced by some process which, whatever it may be, looks like lithograph and thereby reinforces the comparison between Low and the lithographers of the old *Charivari* of Paris—Gavarni and Daumier and their colleagues. They are *illustrations* in the literal sense of the word—pictures of the inside and of the outside of things at the same time.' (Review of 'Low's Russian Sketchbook'—*New Statesman and Nation*, Dec. 10, 1932).[1]

What one tried to point out, and Maynard could not understand, was that no two artists—to be for a moment polite and dishonest—could be much more unalike than Daumier and Low. To begin with, Low is not an artist. He possesses a prodigious knack of inventing visual equivalents for political situations and ideas; and ekes out their meaning with tags which have often the neatness of epigrams. It is a remarkable gift. But those equivalents have no æsthetic value—no value in themselves. The line is as smart and insensitive as the prose of a penny-a-liner. Daumier, who was one of the great draughtsmen of the nineteenth century, lacked entirely that gift which in old days made us buy the *Evening Standard* to see what Low was up to. Having made a beautiful drawing, which might or might not suggest some crude bit of social or political criticism, Daumier as often as not, could think of no legend to put under it. The drawing, you see, was not an illustration of something else but a work of art complete in itself. So he left the business of putting in the patter to Philipon or some other clever fellow in the office.

[1]Gladly I take this opportunity of thanking Mr. Kingsley Martin, the editor of *The New Statesman*, who was kind enough to have this review hunted down and transcribed for my benefit.

This distinction to Maynard seemed fanciful, as it must seem to anyone who has no real feeling for visual art. Even in literature his untutored judgment was not to be trusted. During the last war he returned from America with a find—a great new novel. He had discovered a modern master, and he had brought the masterpiece home with him. It was Bemelmans' 'Now I lay me down to sleep', a piece of comicality that might, or might not, while away an hour in the train.

That Maynard Keynes has benefited all the arts by the creation of the Arts Council is a title to glory and a notorious fact which proves nothing contrary to what was said in the last paragraph. It would prove, if further proof were needed, that he was one of those uncommon human beings who have devoted great powers of organisation to good purposes. Maynard's gifts were always at the service of civilization, and by long and affectionate association with artists —do not forget that Lady Keynes was a brilliant ballerina and an interesting actress—he came to realise acutely that of civilization the arts are an essential ingredient. Also this achievement, the creation of the Arts Council in time of war, of a war in which he was playing an important and exhausting part, proves—but again what need of proof?—his boundless energy and versatility, as well as his capacity for making something solid and durable out of a hint. God forbid that anyone should imagine that I am suggesting that it was I who gave the hint. At that time anxious questionings as to the future of the arts in a more or less socialist state were to be heard on all sides. I drag myself into the picture only because I recall a conversation with Maynard which led to my writing, at his suggestion, an article in *The New Statesman* of which, at that time, he was part-proprietor and, unless I mistake, a director. My argument was that, much as I disliked the idea of a Ministry of Fine Arts, the creation of such a Ministry would be, when private patronage had been destroyed by economic egalitarianism, the only means of saving the arts from extinction. The argument was neither striking nor novel; what was remarkable was that Maynard, in the midst of his preoccupations, should not only have devised but realised an institution which might nourish the arts without handing them over to civil servants and politicians. So far his contrivance has worked and worked well. Whether it will continue to evade the embrace of death—of politicians I mean—remains to be seen.

Those who have said that Maynard Keynes had no æsthetic sense may seem to have forgotten his prose. He had a fine, lucid style in which he could state persuasively and wittily the interesting things he had in mind. When he attempted to express the more delicate shades of feeling or to make a picture out of observations rather than ideas, he was, in my opinion, less convincing. Those famous portraits of Clemenceau, Wilson and Lloyd-George have never seemed to me quite the masterpieces they have seemed to other, and perhaps better, judges. They are lively and telling but scarcely subtle I think. To my taste his best book is *Essays in Persuasion*, and the best portrait he ever drew that of Alfred Marshall. In that long biographical notice, reprinted in *Essays in*

Biography, his knowledge and his culture, which, though limited, had been garnered and sifted by an extraordinarily powerful understanding, are most skilfully employed to enlighten what in other hands might have appeared a dull subject. The result, if not precisely beautiful, is more than pleasing: in the exact sense of the word it is admirable.

I said that his culture was limited: such judgments are always relative, and perhaps I should try to be more explicit. As has been intimated, in the visual arts his taste was anything but sure and his knowledge amounted to nothing. Some believe he appreciated music, but I have never discovered the foundations of their belief. Literature is another matter. At Eton Maynard had been reared on the classics, and of the Greek and Latin authors remembered as much as clever people who have enjoyed what are called the advantages of a public school education can be expected to remember. I have heard that he was a fair German scholar, but of that I cannot speak. He had very little French and no Italian. Of English he had read much, both verse and prose. He liked poetry; but he enjoyed it as a well educated man of affairs rather than as an artist or an æsthete. One had only to hear him read aloud —and he was fond of reading poetry aloud—to feel that the content was what he really cared for. His commerce with the English historians would have been more profitable if his memory had been more retentive. He had a capacity for forgetting, and for muddling, dates and figures, that was astonishing and sometimes rather tiresome—tiresome because, with his invincible cocksureness, he could not dream of admitting that he mistook. To the end of his life he continued to study—or perhaps, towards the end, merely to take an interest in—mathematics and philosophy. Presumably he understood Wittgenstein as well as anyone understood him—except Professor Ayer. He never called himself a Logical Positivist. Of his economic theories and constructions, that is to say of the great work of his life, I am too ignorant to speak. I should be able to say more about his theory of Probability than that it served him ill at Monte Carlo, since in the years before the first war I often heard him talk about it. And after that war, when he took up the manuscript of his old disertation with a view to making a book, he would—I suppose because we were living in the same house— occasionally hand me a much corrected sheet saying —such was his lack of memory—'can you remember what I meant by that?' Alas, figures and symbols had crept into the argument and my miserable inaptitude for sums made me unhelpful. Anyhow I am not equipped to criticise so abstruse a theory, but I understand that Ramsay made a rent which caused all the stitches to run.

I dare say most readers will think I have said enough to disprove my statement that Maynard's culture was limited. Maybe I used the wrong word and should have said 'provincial'. To explain what I mean by that, perhaps I may be allowed to draw on my homely but vivid memories. At Charleston it was our habit to sit after dinner in an oblate semi-circle before a curious fire-place, devised and constructed by Roger Fry to heat with logs a particularly chilly room: strange to say, it did. Each of us would be reading his or her book, and someone was sure to be reading French. Also it so happened that, just after the old war, stimulated I think by Aldous Huxley, I had become interested in the life and through the life the plays of Alfieri; wherefore, Alfieri leading on, I might be reading some early nineteenth century Italian. Thus, towards bed-time, could spring up talk about French or Italian ways of thinking, feeling and living. In such discussions one could not but be struck by Maynard's inability to see a foreign country from inside. France, Italy, America even, he saw them all from the white cliffs of Dover, or, to be more exact, from Whitehall or King's combination room. Compared with (say) Roger Fry, who was often of the company, he seemed ludicrously provincial. And that may be what I had in mind when I called his culture limited.

In spite of all the little annoying things that have stuck in my memory, my recollection of Maynard, vivid and persistent, is that of a delightful companion. I miss him; and I understand the feelings of those who more than miss, of those for whom the wound caused by his death never quite heals and may at any moment become painful. What I miss is his conversation. It was brilliant: that is an obvious thing to say but it is the right thing. In the highest degree he possessed that ingenuity which turns commonplaces into paradoxes and paradoxes into truisms, which discovers—or invents—similarities and differences, and associates disparate ideas—that gift of amusing and surprising with which very clever people, and only very clever, can by conversation give a peculiar relish to life. He had a witty intellect and a verbal knack. In argument he was bewilderingly quick, and unconventional. His comment on any subject under discussion, even on a subject about which he knew very little, was apt to be so lively and original that one hardly stopped to enquire whether it was just. But in graver mood, if asked to explain some technical business, which to the amateur seemed incomprehensible almost, he would with good-humoured ease make the matter appear so simple that one knew not whether to be more amazed at his intelligence or one's own stupidity. In moments such as these I felt sure that Maynard was the cleverest man I had ever met; also, at such moments, I sometimes felt, unreasonably no doubt, that he was an artist.

That Maynard Keynes was a great man is generally admitted; but in private life no one could have been less 'great-manish'. He was never pompous. His greatness no doubt revealed itself most impressively in economics—the work of his life—in organisation and negotiation; but of greatness in such matters I am not competent to speak. Nor yet, alas! am I entitled to speak of what to some was his most memorable quality: for me his cleverness was what counted most, but to a few privileged men and women who knew him through and through his supreme virtue was his deeply affectionate nature. He liked a great many people of all sorts and to them he gave pleasure, excitement and good counsel; but his dearest friends he loved passionately and faithfully and, odd as it may sound, with a touch of humility.

V

ROGER FRY

'YOU knew him well, why don't you give us your picture of him?' said an American friend with whom I was talking about Roger Fry. Because, said I, Virginia Woolf wrote a biography which, besides being as complete an account of Fry's life as for the present it would be seemly to publish, happens to be a masterpiece: I have no notion of entering into competition with one of the great writers of my age. Of course I knew well enough that what my friend had in mind was something utterly unlike Mrs. Woolf's biography; what he expected of me was an appetising lecture, fifty-five minutes of lively gossip, a chapter from my unpublished memoirs. But here again a lion was in the way: for though, as a matter of fact, I did jot down soon after Fry's death, for the amusement of my friends and his, a handful of anecdotes intended to illustrate just one facet of his nature—the lovably absurd, I felt that to enjoy these fantastic tales it was necessary to have known the hero and to have known him well. Now Virginia Woolf made us know him so well that she was able to avail herself of my collection—which was of course at her service—dropping delicately here an absurdity there an extravagance with telling effect: but I am not Virginia Woolf. I cannot bring the dead to life, and so I cannot effectively retell my own stories. All I can do is to give, or try to give, the impression made on me by the man, the critic and the painter, drawing more on my recollection of what he said and did than on what he published, which is after all accessible to all and I hope familiar to most. For his ideas I must go sometimes to his books; but of his character and gifts I will try to give an account based on what I remember of his sayings and doings.

'How did Roger Fry strike you?' That, I suppose, is the question. It is not easily answered. That fine, old sport of analysing characters and reducing them to their component qualities or humours is out of fashion, and was, I admit, as a method, unsubtle. Still, no one who knew Roger is likely to quarrel with me if I say that some of the things that come first to mind when one thinks of him are intelligence, sweetness, ardour and sensibility; nor I believe will it be denied that one of the first things to catch the attention of anyone who was coming acquainted with him was likely to be his prodigious and varied knowledge. To be sure, the very first thing that struck me was his appearance. He was tall—about six foot I dare say; but did not look his height. Maybe he stooped a little; he was well made, by no means lanky, anyhow he certainly did not give the impression of a very tall man. What one noticed were his eyes which were both round and penetrating—an uncommon combination—and were made to appear rounder by large circular goggles. One noticed his hair too—once black, I believe, but greyish when I met him—which, long, rebellious and silky, somehow accentuated his features which, in profile at all events, were very sharply defined. He was clean shaven. There was something the air of a judge about him, but still more the air of one who is perpetually surprised by life—as indeed he was. At moments he reminded me of a highly sagacious rocking-horse. He wore good clothes badly. Obviously they had been made by the right tailor, but there was always something wrong with them. It might be a too decorative tie fashioned out of some unlikely material, or a pair of yellow brown sandals worn when black shoes would have been appropriate. His hats were peculiar; broad-brimmed, round, Quakerish and becoming. Only in full evening dress—white tie, white waistcoat, boiled shirt and collar—did he appear smart. Then, with his silvery hair carefully brushed, he looked infinitely distinguished.

So much for the impression made at first meeting. Acquaintance ripening to friendship, you would probably note a restless activity of mind and body. Ardent he was, as I have said, intelligent, sensitive, sweet, cultivated and erudite: these qualities and attainments revealed themselves sooner or later, and soon rather than late, to everyone who came to know him, and of them I must speak first. But what charmed his intimate friends almost as much as his rare qualities was his boundless gullibility: of that I shall speak later.

I have said that his knowledge was what might well have struck you in the beginning. One was surprised by the amount he knew before one realised that it was a mere means to something far more precious—to culture in the best sense of the word. Roger Fry was what Bacon calls 'a full man'; but his various erudition was only a means to thought and feeling and the enrichment of life. Knowledge he knew added immensely to the fun of the fair, enabling one to make the most of any odd fact that comes one's way by seeing it in relation to other facts and to theories and so fitting it into the great jig-saw puzzle. But he never cared much to be given a result unless he could learn how that result had been obtained; and therein you will recognise one of the essential qualifications of a scholarly critic. At Cambridge his studies had been scientific: that is something to have in mind for it helps to an understanding of the man, his merits and some of his defects. He took a first in the Natural Science tripos. To do that, I am assured, requires more than smattering a little Botany and cutting up a few frogs: to have done it is, I suspect, to have given the mind a bent which the most varied and thrilling experiences of later life will hardly rectify.

I shall ask you to bear in mind, then, that Roger Fry was a man of science by training and to some extent by temper. I shall not ask you to bear in mind that he was intelligent and lovable, because intelligence and charm are the very oil and pigment in which the picture of his life is to be painted. These qualities, I hope, will make themselves felt without demonstration as my tale proceeds. His old friends will not be surprised if I do not insist on them; what may surprise some is that I did not put first among his qualities, Sensibility. That Fry had acquired exquisite sensibility was clear to all who knew him or read his writings or listened to his lectures, and clearer still to those who worked with him. To watch, or rather catch, him—for in such matters his methods were summary—disposing of a foolish attribution, was to realise just how convincing a decision based on trained sensibility and knowledge can be. I have seen a little dealer, with all due ceremony, reverence and precaution, produce from a triply locked safe what purported to be a Raphael Madonna; I have seen Fry give it one glance or two and heard him say sweetly but firmly 'an eighteenth-century copy and a bad one at that'; and I have seen the dealer, himself for the moment convinced, fling the picture back into the safe without so much as bothering to lock the door. Such was the force of Fry's sensibility—trained sensibility supported by intelligence and knowledge. His possession of that has never been called in question so far as I know. What perhaps he did not possess, in such abundance at all events, was that innate sensibility, that hankering after beauty, that liking for art which resembles a liking for alcohol, that 'gusto' as Hazlitt would have called it, which is the best gift of many second- and third-rate painters and of some critics even— Théophile Gautier for instance. In a later chapter I shall try to recall the joy of wandering about Paris, a boy just down from Cambridge, with the Canadian, J. W. Morrice—a typical good second-rate painter (first-rate almost)—and of being made to feel beauty in the strangest places; not in cafés and music-halls only (in those days, about 1904, the classic haunts of beauty), but on hoardings and in shop-windows, in itinerant musicians singing sentimental romances, in smart frocks and race-meetings and arias by Gounod, in penny-steamers and sunsets and military uniforms, at the *Opéra comique* even, and even at the

Comédie française. With Roger Fry I have been privileged to travel in many parts of Europe, and from him I have learnt to discover uncharted subtleties and distinguish between fine shades of expression; but I do not think he could have found beauty where Morrice found it. Perhaps Roger possessed in the highest degree sensibility of a methodical kind, what I have called 'trained sensibility'; whereas Morrice had the sensibility of an artist—innate. I do not know.

His first approach to art was so hampered by family tradition, lofty and puritan, that it was I dare say inevitable that he should make some false starts and fall into some pits from which a normal, barbarous upbringing might have saved him. Also the climate of Cambridge in the ' 'eighties', and even later, was not altogether favourable to growth of the æsthetic sense. Also he was reading science. All this I take into account: and all this notwithstanding I do feel, re-reading the story of his early years, that his blunders of commission and omission, his baseless enthusiasms and blind spots, were not those of a very young artist but of an intellectual at any age. Assuredly the admirations and anathemas of the very young are never to be brought up against them; but in 1892 Fry was twenty-six and, what is more, had for some time been an art-student, which makes it hard to believe that, had sensibility been innate, he could have spent months in Paris—at Jullian's too— without feeling a thrill for the Impressionists and could have found in the Luxembourg nothing more exciting than Bastien Lepage.[1]

[1]It should be remembered, however, that the Caillebotte collection had not yet been installed.

I spoke of family tradition lofty and puritan: the puritan strain in Roger's character his friends might like but could not ignore. To his hours of abandon even it gave an air of revolt. His paganism was protestant—a protest against puritanism. Intellectually the freest of men, and almost indecently unprejudiced, he made one aware of a slight wrench, the ghost of a struggle, when he freed his mind to accept or condone what his forbears would have called 'vile pleasures'. It is on this streak of puritanism the devil's advocate will fasten when Roger comes up, as come up he will, for canonisation. He was open-minded, but he was not fair-minded. For though, as I have said, he was magnificently unprejudiced, he was not unprincipled; and he had a way of being sure that while all his own strong feelings were principles those of others, when they happened to cross his, were unworthy prejudices. Thanks to his puritanical upbringing he could sincerely regard his principles as in some sort the will of God. From which it followed that anyone who opposed them must have said, like Satan, 'Evil be thou my good'. People who happened not to agree with him found this annoying.

Few of us are all of a metal; most, as Dryden puts it, are 'dashed and brewed with lies'. The best founded even are flawed with some disharmony. The cup is just troubled with an 'aliquid amari', and the bitterness will now and then catch in the throat and spoil the flavour of life as it goes down. A tang of puritanism was in Roger's cup: it was barely appreciable, yet to it I believe can be traced most of his defects as man and critic. Not all: there are defects that can be traced to his scientific training and temper, but here there is gain to record as well as loss. The pure unscientific æsthete is a sensationalist. He feels first; only later, if he happens to be blest—or curst—with a restless intellect, will he condescend to reason about his feelings. It would be false and silly to suggest that Roger Fry's emotions were at the service of his theories; but he was too good a natural philosopher to enjoy seeing a theory pricked by a fact. Now the mere æsthete is for ever being bowled over by facts: the facts that upset him being as a rule works of art which according to current doctrine ought not to come off but which somehow or other do (e.g. the Houses of Parliament or the works of Kipling). The æsthete, sensationalist that he is, rather likes being knocked down by an outsider. He picks himself up and goes on his way rejoicing in an adventure. Roger Fry did not altogether like it. He entered a gallery with a gereralisation in his head—a generalisation which, up to that moment, was, or should be, a complete explanation of art. He was not the man to deny facts, and he was much too sensitive to overlook the sort I have in mind; but I do think he was inclined to give marks to pictures which, because they were right in intention, ought to have been right in achievement, and sometimes, I think, he was rather unwilling to recognise the patent but troublesome beauty of works that seemed to be sinning against the light. Nine times out of ten this tendency towards injustice was due to a puritanical aversion from charm, and to counter it the spirit of science had made him magnificently open-minded. He was the most open-minded man I ever met: the only one indeed who tried to practise that fundamental precept of science—that nothing should be assumed to be true or false until it has been put to the test. This made him willing to hear what anyone had to say even about questions on which he was a recognised authority, even though 'anyone' might be a schoolboy or a housemaid: this also made him a champion gull—but of that later. Had he fallen in with a schoolboy—a manifestly sincere and eager schoolboy—in the Arena Chapel at Padua, and had that boy confessed that he could see no merit in the frescos, Roger would have argued the question on the spot, panel by panel: and this he would have done in no spirit of amiable complacency. Always supposing the boy to be serious and ardent, the great critic would have been attentive to the arguments and objections of the small iconoclast: convinced, I suppose, he would have modified his judgment and, if necessary, recast his æsthetic.

About that æsthetic, which gave him so much trouble, I shall soon have a word to say. But first let me give an example of open-mindedness and integrity which will, I hope, make some amends for what I have said or shall say concerning his slightly biased approach to works of art. Always he had disliked Indian art: it offended his sense of reasonableness and his taste. Late in life, having enjoyed opportunities of studying more and better examples may be, or perhaps merely having studied more happily and freely examples that were always within his reach, he changed his mind. That done, the next thing to do was to 'own up'. And 'own up' he did in a discriminating lecture. When you remember that at the time of writing this palinode Roger Fry was getting on for seventy and was the foremost critic in Europe, I think you will agree that he gave proof of considerable open-mindedness and a lesson to us all. The scientific spirit is not without its uses in the appreciation of the fine arts: neither is character.

Indeed he was open-minded; which is not to say, as jealous fools were at one time fond of saying, that he was a weather-cock, slave to every gust of enthusiasm. It is a memorable fact, to which Sir Kenneth Clark sorrowfully calls attention in his preface to *Last Lectures*, that, try as he would, Fry could never bring himself greatly to admire Greek sculpture. He would have been glad to admire it: for Greek civilization, for the Greek view and way of life, for Greek prose and verse, philosophy and science, he felt what all intelligent and well educated people must feel. He realised that Athens was man's masterpiece. And so, towards the end of his life, he went with three friends —one an accomplished Hellenist and all highly intelligent—to see whether he could not prove himself wrong. The will to admire was there: but honesty, but fidelity to his personal reaction, proved the stronger. He found Greek sculpture, whether archaic or of what is called 'the great age', comparatively dull. And he said so.

Roger Fry was troubled by æsthetics; anyone who cares for art yet cannot keep his intellect quiet must be. Roger cared passionately, and positively enjoyed analysing his emotions: also he did it better, I think, than anyone had done it before. Having analysed he went on to account for his feelings, and got into that fix which everyone gets into who makes the attempt: *experto credite*. Art is almost as wide as life; and to

invent a hypothesis which shall comprehend it may
be as difficult, just as it may appear as simple, as to
explain the universe. The place where Roger stuck
is where we all stick. There is a constant in art just
as, once upon a time, there was supposed to be a
constant in life. I have a notion they called it 'C':
anyhow that was a long time ago. But I feel pretty
sure that in those far off days the difference between
Organic and Inorganic was determined by the presence or absence of a definable somewhat; and still it
is permissible to say that a work of art cannot exist
unless there be present what I used to call 'significant
form', and you may call by any name you please—
provided that what you mean by your name is a
combination of lines and colours, or of notes, or of
words, in itself moving, i.e. moving without reference
to the outside world. Only, to say that, is no more to
answer the question 'What is art?' than to chatter
about 'C' is, or ever was, to answer the question
'What is life?' Renoir, painting pictures of girls and
fruit, concentrated his attention exclusively on their
forms and colours. But implicit in those forms and
colours, for Renoir inseparable from them, was appe-
tisingness—the feeling that girls are good to kiss and
peaches to eat. Easy enough to see that when a
painter sets out to make you feel that his girls would
be nice to kiss he ceases to be an artist and becomes
a pornographer or a sentimentalist. Renoir never
dreams of trying to make you feel anything of that
sort; he is concerned only with saying what he feels
about forms and colours. Nevertheless, he does feel,
consciously or subconsciously, embedded in those
forms and colours, deliciousness. All that he feels he

expresses. Now all that an artist expresses is part of his work of art. The problem is turning nasty, you perceive; complicate it, multiply instances and diversify them, and you will be near where Roger stuck. He never quite swallowed my impetuous doctrine—Significant Form first and last, alone and all the time; he knew too much, and such raw morsels stuck in his scientific throat. He came near swallowing it once; but always he was trying to extend his theory to cover new difficulties—difficulties presented, not only by an acute and restless intellect, but by highly trained sensibility playing on vast experience. Need I say that his difficulties were always ahead of his explanations? In wrestling with them he raised a number of interesting questions; better still—far better—he threw a flood of brilliant light on art in general and on particular works. Read again that masterly chapter in *Transformations* called 'Some Questions in Æsthetics', a matter of fifty pages, in which he goes deeper into the subject than anyone had gone before or has gone since—I am not forgetting Max Eastman whom I greatly admire. You will find the destructive criticism entirely satisfying; you will be enlightened by the analysis of æsthetic experience; you will enjoy seeing the finest mince-meat made of Mr. Richards's simple-minded psychological explanations, which boil down to the absurd conclusion that our responses to works of art are the same as our responses to life; and when it comes to justification let Fry speak for himself:

'As to the value of the æsthetic emotion—it is clearly infinitely removed from those ethical values to which Tolstoy would have confined it. It seems to be as remote from actual life and its practical utilities as the most useless mathematical theorem. One can say only that those who experience it feel it to have a peculiar quality of "reality" which makes it a matter of infinite importance in their lives. Any attempt I might make to explain this would probably land me in the depths of mysticism. On the edge of that gulf I stop.' (*Vision and Design*, p. 199).

Certainly his wrestlings helped to give muscle to the body of Fry's criticism; but to the building of that body went many rare aliments—trained sensibility, intellect, peculiar knowledge, wide general culture, the scientific spirit and honour. Virginia Woolf speaks of 'his power of making pictures real and art important'. Words could not give better a sense of just what it was Roger Fry did for my generation and the next. Having learnt to feel intensely the beauty and glory and wonder of a work of visual art he could, so to speak, unhook his emotion and hold it under, I will not say a microscope, but an uncommonly powerful pair of spectacles. That done, he could find, and sometimes invent, words to convey feelings and analyses of feelings into the apprehension of the reader—or listener: it was even better to be a listener than a reader. I am not thinking of those unforgettable conversations and discussions before particular works of art in churches and galleries, but of his lectures. Roger Fry's lectures were his best critical performances: he was the perfect lecturer almost. And the lecture with slides is the perfect medium for pictorial exegesis, permitting, as it does, the lecturer to bring before the eyes of his audience images of the objects about which he is speaking, thinking and feeling. To hear a lecture by Roger Fry was the next best thing to sight-seeing in his company. He stuck but loosely to his text, allowing himself to be inspired by whatever was on the screen. It was from a sensation to a word. Almost one could watch him thinking and feeling.

To say the excruciatingly difficult things Fry set himself to say he was obliged to work language pretty hard. In my opinion he worked it well. His prose was lucid and lively, and on occasions he could be delightfully witty and verbally felicitous. His biographer glances, critically but affectionately, at his habit of repeating favourite phrases. The fault is unavoidable in the prose of an art-critic since there is no vocabulary of art-criticism. If such terms as 'plastic sequence', 'plastic unity', 'inner life', 'structural planes' keep cropping up, that is because they are the only symbols available for subtle and complex things which themselves keep cropping up. It is essential to understanding that readers or listeners should know precisely what the critic is referring to; and only by repeatedly describing in the same terms the same concepts can he hope to give these terms anything like generally accepted significance. To some extent the art-critic must create his own vocabulary.

Writing, as a fine art, was Roger's foible. Of prose and verse rhythms he was indistinctly aware; but he liked spinning theories about them. Of his translations of Mallarmé the less said the better: the one significant thing about them is that he believed them to be adequate. They have made me think of Bentley editing Milton; for, after all, Bentley was a great, a very great critic, and in some ways understood Greek poetry as it never had been understood by a modern. Having named Milton I find myself thinking of some gibberish Roger once wrote—for the benefit of intimate friends only—gibberish which did possess recognisable similarity of sound with the *Ode on the Nativity* but did not possess what he firmly believed it to possess, i.e. all, or almost all, the merits of the original. The gibberish was, of course, deliberate gibberish—a collection of sounds so far as possible without meaning. It was highly ingenious, and I am bound to reckon the theory behind it pretty, seeing that it was much the same as one I had myself propounded years earlier as an explanation of visual art. Only, at the time Roger's experiment was made we were deep in the 'twenties' and the fine frenzy of Post-Impressionism was a thing of the past. There was now no controversial axe to grind. Simply, Roger liked the theory because he felt it was one in the eye for 'magic'. It came from the heart rather than the head and he wanted to believe it. Now it was this gibberish, and his opinion of it, and the passion with which he defended his opinion, that finally opened my eyes to a truth which had, I suppose, always been plain to those who did not love him: Roger's feeling for poetry was puritanical. The charm, the romance, the imagery, the glamour, the magic offended the quaker that was in him; wherefore he was very willing to believe that all that signified could be reduced to clean, dry bones.

Having said so much about writing and lecturing, I must say something, I suppose, about painting. It is an unenviable task; for, preposterous as it must seem to those who know him only by his achievement, Roger Fry took his painting more seriously than he took his criticism. It was the most important thing in his life, or at any rate he thought it was. He said so and his friends were bound to believe him; yet some of them wondered: surely he knew that he was the best critic alive, and, at the bottom of his heart, can he have believed that he was a very good painter? He knew that those whose opinion he valued did not think so. To me it seems that his early work, especially his water-colours and paintings on silk, are his happiest productions. They are frankly eclectic; the influence of some master, of some English water-colourist as a rule, being acknowledged at every turn. But in most of these works—things done before 1910 shall we say?—there are pleasing qualities which later I seek in vain. Unashamed, in those unregenerate days, he could utilise his knowledge, and exploit his taste, the delicacy of his perceptions, his sleight of hand. All these assets contributed to a tentative style which did in some sort express a part of his nature. The Post-Impressionist revolution which set free so many of his latent capacities overwhelmed these modest virtues. It set free his capacity for living and enjoying, but it did no good to his painting. On the contrary, that movement which was to liberate the creative powers of all those young and youngish artists who possessed any powers worth liberating, that movement of which in this country he was the animator, did Fry's painting harm, driving it into uncongenial ways. He tried to paint in a manner which he understood admirably and explained brilliantly but could not make his own. No longer decked in the rather antiquated finery which had fitted his temper on one side at any rate, his painting gift appeared naked, and we perceived to our dismay that it amounted to next to nothing. His very energy and quickness, qualities elsewhere profitable, here served him ill. He worked too fast. Neither had he that ruminating enjoyment which lingers over a subject till the last oozings of significance have been tasted, nor yet the patience which will elaborate a design to its last possibilities. I have seen him, out of sheer conscientiousness, or in some desperate hope of a miraculous revelation, work on at a picture to which he knew he could add nothing, for all the world like an examination-candidate who has written all he knows and vainly strives to improve the appearance of his paper by writing it all over again. Roger knew that he had added nothing. Maybe he knew too much.

Roger Fry was a good, though impatient, craftsman, proper of his hands and quick to learn a trade. His best productions in this sort are the white pots and plates he made for the Omega; and it is to be hoped that a few will be preserved in some public collection, for they grow rare. But no sooner did he think it necessary to embellish a chair or a table or a chest of drawers, to beautify a curtain, a lampshade or a frock, than something went wrong. There must have been a devil, I have sometimes fancied, a demon born of puritanism and pampered in young 'artistic' days, which lurked in his sub-consciousness and on favourable occasions poked up its nose. At any rate, in all that he did for the Omega, with the exception of those plain white pots and plates, I taste an unpleasant flavour—a flavour redolent of 'artistry'. That was the devil's revenge; and perhaps it was this same evil spirit that forbade Fry the paradise of creation. From that delectable country he was excluded; he could not reach the frontiers because where art begins some perverse sub-consciousness or self-consciousness arrested him. What was it precisely? I hardly know. Could he have believed—no, he could not have believed nor thought either—but could he have hoped, in some dark corner of his being inaccessible to reason, that style could be imposed? A horrid fancy: that way lie art guilds and gowns, sandals, homespun and welfare-work, and at the end yawns an old English tea-room. If Roger had finished a picture before he had begun a work of art, that may have been because he could not practise what he preached so well—that in creating all the horses must be driven abreast, that you cannot hitch on style or beauty as an ostler used to hitch on a tracer. And if I am asked why Roger Fry's painting seems dead, all I can say is what Renoir said when asked whether art comes from the head or the heart: '*des couilles*' he replied.

But if Roger Fry was not an artist, he was one of the most remarkable men of his age, besides being one of the most lovable. This his biographer has established; his other friends can but bring a few flowers to the monument and cherish the inscription. I first met him appropriately enough in the morning train from Cambridge to King's Cross. It was early in 1910, a moment at which Fry was in a sense beginning a new life. The tragedy in which the old had ended, the courage and devotion with which that tragedy had been fought and for a while warded off,

Mrs. Woolf has most movingly recounted. In 1910 Roger Fry was in his forty-fifth year: one life was ending and a new, and perhaps more exciting, about to begin. Indeed, it was a moment at which everyone felt excitement in the air: had not I—even I—just sat down to describe the general state of affairs in an *opus* to bear the pregnant title *The New Renaissance*, an *opus* of which the bit I did publish three years later, a book called *Art*, would have formed a mere chapter. Certainly there was stir: in Paris and London at all events there was a sense of things coming right, though whether what we thought was coming could properly be described as a 'renaissance' now seems to me doubtful. The question is academic: as usual the statesmen came to the rescue, and Mr. Asquith, Sir Edward Grey and M. Viviani declared war on Germany. But in 1910 only statesmen dreamed of war, and quite a number of wide-awake people imagined the good times were just round the corner. Miracles seemed likely enough to happen; but when Roger Fry told me that morning in the train that he proposed to show the British public the work of the newest French painters, I told him that I would be proud to help in any way I could but that his scheme was fantastic. Not that there was any question of my being of serious use—Roger never needed an *État-Major*; but as I had written in praise of Cézanne and Gauguin and other 'revolutionaries' he thought I might as well give a hand. Anyhow, I was put on a committee which did nothing, and late that summer I joined Roger and Desmond MacCarthy in Paris: in the autumn opened the first Post-Impressionist exhibition.

Of this exhibition and the next Fry was, as everyone knows, the original and moving spirit: 'as everyone knew' perhaps I should have said. For lately a
story has been put about that it was not Roger Fry
who introduced the Post-Impressionist masters to the
British public and stimulated that enthusiasm for
their work which persists. Even it has been suggested
that the credit should go to Mr. Samuel Courtauld,
which is of course sheer nonsense. Far from being a
pioneer, Sam Courtauld—I speak with some authority as a fairly close friend—was a little behind the
times. It was in 1922 that he began to collect Post-
Impressionist paintings; before that date he had
been buying work of quite another kind—pictures
by D. Y. Cameron for instance. In 1911 I do not
think Roger Fry knew him; but before 1920 at latest
he (Courtauld) had been strongly urged by Roger
Fry, or at Fry's instigation, to buy pictures by
Cézanne, Van Gogh and Gauguin, which already
were beyond the reach of the small collectors who
coveted them.

Mr. Douglas Cooper in a valuable introduction
to his catalogue of the Courtauld Collection—a
masterpiece of exact and brilliant scholarship—has
inexplicably misjudged the public reaction to the
Post-Impressionist exhibitions of 1910–11–12 and
consequently has misunderstood the sentiment of the
succeeding decade. Of the first exhibition he writes:
'But today one cannot help feeling that it was an
unfortunate exhibition, for it presented a distorted
view of Post-Impressionist developments and, by
virtue of its own inconsistencies, had the effect of
frightening the English public away from rather

than of encouraging it to take an active interest in modern French art.'

This is not true. Rich collectors, directors and their trustees may well have been frightened—Mr. Courtauld himself was frightened I dare say—but the younger members of the art-loving public were for the most part wildly enthusiastic. And the enthusiasm endured. During the next ten years, war notwithstanding, the interest in modern French art never flagged; also throughout those years Roger Fry was the animator. When, immediately after the war Sir Osbert Sitwell brought over from Paris a scratch lot of pictures collected by Zborowski, the supply hardly met the demand. For that matter, already at the first and second Post-Impressionist exhibitions almost all the cheaper pictures found buyers. And here, maybe, we touch on one of the causes of Mr. Cooper's misconception. He was writing of the Courtauld collection and consequently thinking of big prices. True it is that rich collectors and trustees of public galleries held aloof till prices had become not big but preposterous; and that, though he did not begin till 1922, Mr. Courtauld was the second, or perhaps the third, in this country to buy expensive Post-Impressionist pictures. Roger Fry was not to blame for that. The art-loving public is not composed exclusively of rich men; chiefly it is composed of men and women of moderate means, and already in 1910 the works of Cézanne, Gauguin and Van Gogh were beyond those means, as, in 1912, were the more important works of Matisse and Picasso. Nevertheless, though not impressive purchasers, the admirers of the Post-Impressionists and of contemporary French painting were enthusiastic and numerous.

Mr. Cooper complains that the first Post-Impressionist exhibition came to the public as a shock. It should have been led up to gradually. Here speaks the historian rather than the art-lover; for though Mr. Cooper loves art he adores chronology, and chronology he feels was slighted. Probably it was. There are scholars who think that exhibitions should be organised for historians rather than amateurs. Roger Fry was not one of them. He was content to show a number of fine pictures and encourage people to enjoy them. They did enjoy them.[1]

One result of the first Post-Impressionist exhibition was that Roger Fry became the animator and advocate of the younger British painters; but not the master. Few young painters mistook him for a master, though to him they looked for advice and encouragement and sometimes for material support. With his fine intellect, culture and persuasive ways he became spokesman for modern art—our representative in the councils of the great; for he could place his word where he would. *The Times* felt bound to print letters from him in large type on the leader page. Even fine ladies, even the Prime Ministress, had to pretend to listen. And, under the wand of the enchanter, with his looks, his voice, his infinite variety and palpable good faith, those who began to listen found themselves becoming converts. It was now, in these last years of peace, that France became

[1]In writing these paragraphs I have made free with a longish review I contributed to *The Times Literary Supplement* (March 26, 1954).

for him what for the rest of his life she remained—
his second country; and there he made friends, deep,
affectionate and charming, who later were to do
much to lighten the gloom of declining years. At
home, too, between 1910 and '14 he was making
friends, some of whom were to grow into close companions and collaborators; and of these most, it is to
be noted, were of a generation younger than his own.
They were, I think, gayer, more ribald, more un-
shockable, more pleasure-loving and less easily impressed by grave airs and fine sentiments than the
friends—whom, by the way, he never lost nor ceased
to love—with whom he had grown to middle age.
It was from these younger people that he learnt to
enjoy shamelessly almost—yes, almost. Their blissful
adiabolism helped him to ignore the nudgings of the
old puritan Nick. And this I like to count some small
return for all they learnt from him. He taught them
much: amongst other things, by combining with an
utterly disinterested and unaffected passion for art a
passion for justice and hatred of cruelty, he made
them aware of the beauty of goodness. That virtue
could be agreeable came as a surprise to some of us.
Like all satisfactory human relationships, these new
friendships were matters of give and take; and I
know who gave most. Nevertheless, between the first
Post-Impressionist exhibition and the first war I have
a notion that Roger Fry changed more than he had
changed in all the years between Cambridge and
that exhibition.

I have suggested that one reason why Roger was
unable to elaborate a work of art and knocked off
too many works of craft was that his boundless en-

ergy induced impatience. This energy, allied with
prodigious strength of will, was terrifying; and it is
not surprising that his enemies, and his friends too
when they chanced to be his victims, called him
ruthless and obstinate; for it is provoking to be
driven straight into a field of standing corn because
your driver cannot admit that his map may be out
of date or that he may have misread it. Of this energy and wilfulness an extract from my unpublished
notes may perhaps give some idea. So, 'I recall a
cold and drizzling Sunday in August: I cannot be
sure of the year. Roger is staying with us at Charleston, convalescent; for, like many exceptionally ro-
bust and energetic men, Roger was a valetudinarian.
I remember hearing my wife say, probably at breakfast, that she suspected him of intending to be motor-
ed some time in the afternoon to Seaford, eight or
nine miles away, where dwelt his curious old friend,
Hindley Smith; but that she, the weather being vile,
the road slippery, the car open and ill-humoured,
had no intention of obliging him. Just before lunch
Frances Marshall (Mrs. Ralph Partridge) who also
was staying with us, and possessed, like my wife,
what most would deem a will of iron, told me she
had a headache and meant, the moment lunch was
over, to slip off to bed, if that could be done without
causing commotion. In any case she was not going
to play chess with Roger. For my part I never cared
about playing chess with Roger; if, by any chance,
one succeeded in some little plot for surprising his
queen or rook—and setting traps is what amuses all
thoroughly bad players such as I—he would dismiss
the strategem as 'uninteresting', retract a series of

moves—generally to his own advantage—and so continue till on scientific and avowable principles he had beaten one to his satisfaction. Anyhow, on this dark and dismal Sunday, lunch finished, Roger sprang to his feet—all invalid that he was he could spring when the occasion seemed to demand action —exclaiming: "Now Frances for a game." And, as soon as Frances had been allowed to lose in a way of which he could approve, again he sprang: "Now, Vanessa, we've just time to go and see Hindley Smith." Vanessa went like a lamb.'

I have spoken of Roger's open-mindedness, of his readiness to listen to anyone he thought sincere: that was fine. His aptitude for discovering sincerity in unlikely places was fine, too, I suppose; but sometimes it landed him in difficulties. Not to mince words, he was a champion gull: gullibility was the laughable and lovable defect of a quality. Stories illustrating this weakness abound; one or two, which I am proud to say, are drawn from my notes, appear in Virginia Woolf's biography. If I venture to impose yet another on your patience, the excuse must be that it illustrates, or at least adumbrates, more than one characteristic.

The scene is laid in a studio in the south of France. It is a cold spring day and we are sitting round a stove drinking tea. Roger has recieved a letter; to be sure he received it several days ago and it has been kept ostentatiously secret ever since. It is from an American book and picture dealer in a small, private way of business. It is highly important and extremely confidential, but Roger must speak or burst. Well, of course the writer wanted money—a good deal of money. Why he wanted so much will appear. In Vienna, in what was rather vaguely termed 'the archives', someone had discovered certain papers. These turned out to be no less than the secret papers of Roger Bacon—and in fact some writings of his, not in the least secret, had been unearthed several months earlier—but these *secret* papers proved beyond doubt that the admirable friar had foreseen everything—flying-machines, motor-cars, telephones, wireless, high explosives, poison gas—all the modern conveniences in short. Now for some reason not very clearly defined these documents were extremely damaging to the Papacy: also the Pope had forbidden their publication. They could be published only in the United States, and there only if some millionaire could be induced to buy them and print at his own expense. Surely Mr. Roger Fry, former adviser to the Metropolitan Museum and to Mr. Pierpont Morgan, would know of a likely purchaser. For until they were purchased these world-shaking documents could not be made public. That was clear; and even when they had been purchased they must be smuggled into America. Such is the influence of the Church.

You might have thought there were other possibilities. At that time Austria herself was a republic under social-democratic government, as was Germany. Russia was just over the way, and there seemed no reason to suppose that something damaging to the Vatican would necessarily be banned in Moscow. Also, there was France, a land of tempered liberty, to say nothing of England. So you might have thought: you would have thought wrong. None of these countries would do: to America the precious papers must be conveyed, though at frightful personal risk and incalculable expense. There indeed they could be printed, but only if rich collectors were sufficiently public-spirited to buy them, *en bloc* or severally; for only when they had been bought and paid for, in dollars, could the picture-dealing bookseller undertake the perilous, but for the future happiness of mankind essential, task of making their contents generally known.

Having told this long story with a long face Roger concluded that something must be done. Vainly was it suggested to him that if safety from the Inquisition were all that was needed there could be no call to go so far afield as Fifth Avenue or Wall Street: besides, was it likely the Pope would consider anything written in the thirteenth century fatal to his prestige in the twentieth? Roger was not to be shaken. He had swallowed the tale, hook, line and sinker. The Jew was an honest Jew, manifestly the victim of priestly intrigue and powerful obscurantism. So to no purpose did I doubt whether anything Roger Bacon might be found to have said was likely to prove more difficult to get round than what had already been published by Bayle or Hume or Voltaire, or, for that matter, Darwin: in vain did I wonder why these manuscripts could not be printed till they had been sold. Roger was not impressed. Only he felt, as one could see, that we were all surprisingly unfair. Indeed he was shocked, as he admitted in a letter, that anyone as intelligent as my son, Julian, should have supported me in my notorious and stupid scepticism.

Inevitably one so gullible and so often gulled grew suspicious—not of the crooks, but of old friends and well meaning acquaintances. To make matters worse, Roger had no turn for practical psychology. A poorer judge of men I have seldom met, and it goes without saying he piqued himself on penetration. He was as ready as Rousseau to believe in *conspirations holbachiques*, and was given to explaining plots which he supposed to have been woven against him, and had in truth been woven in his own imagination, by facts and motives which his friends knew to be non-existent. Does this sound sinister? It was not; for his attention could be diverted with the greatest ease from private grievances to general ideas or, better still, to particular events—in plain words to gossip. In both he delighted; also his mind was far too nimble, his capacity for enjoyment too keen, his taste too pure, his sense of fun too lively, for him to dwell long on petty troubles. He was not much like Rousseau after all. But suspicious he was, and in his fits of suspicion unjust. He could be as censorius as an ill-conditioned judge: possibly the trait was hereditary. Then it was that the puritan came out from hiding undisguised and made him believe that those who differed from him must be actuated by the foulest motives. In such moods it was that he suspected those who opposed him of having said, like Satan, 'evil be thou my good'; also, it seems to me, these moods grew more frequent with the years, bringing with them a perceptible loss of magnanimity. So it seems to me. Or was it that some of his old friends were growing touchy? That explanation is admissible too.

In this discursive chapter I hope to have given some idea of the qualities that made Roger Fry one of the most remarkable men of his age. A combination of intellect and sensibility, extensive culture not in the arts only but in history and science as well, dexterous manipulation of a fine instrument, and an unrivalled power of getting close in words to thoughts and feelings, made him indisputably our first critic. In fact he was more than the first critic of the age; so far as I can judge from my readings in three languages he was one of the best writers on visual art that ever lived. There may be Russians or Germans who have responded more delicately and analysed their responses more acutely, who have contrived to come nearer the heart of the matter; if so, I shall be glad to study their works as soon as they have been translated. Add to these gifts, which were as one may say open to the public, those with which in private he charmed his friends, a playful intellect for instance, free fancy and a sense of fun, along with taste in food and wine, and you have beside a great critic a rare companion. Men I have known who possessed tempers to me more congenial, but none better equipped to please generally. His was, on the whole, a happy disposition, and a cause of happiness in others. One permanent anxiety beset him: it was the child of his virtues. He dreaded, especially during the last years of his life, the collapse of civilization. For civilization he cared nobly; and the prevalence of its mortal enemies—fanaticism, superstition, dogmatism, unreasonableness, the cult of violence and stupidity, contempt of truth and the ways of truth—dismayed him. In naming these vices I have indicated his virtues, which were their contraries. He was a man of many virtues; what is more, in practice he contrived to make them amiable.

VI

VIRGINIA WOOLF

THAT I should have been amongst the first, perhaps the very first, to write a full dress article on Virginia Woolf is neither surprising nor important. I believe it was published in America, possibly in *Vanity Fair* under Frank Crowninshield's rule; but I am not sure. Because I should like to be sure, I mention the matter at the very beginning of this chapter. I should like to know to whom I ought to apologise for making free with his or her property. I have lost track of the thing; and all I can discover is a dirty manuscript written presumably in 1922 or 23 since it ends with an elaborate criticism of *Jacob's Room*, described as 'Mrs. Woolf's latest novel'. For the rest, it is a longish piece of five thousand words or so, but was I dare say cut down for publication. I should be amused to see how it looks in print, though I cannot say that in manuscript it reads particularly well: maybe at the time it seemed interesting because so little was known of the subject. Be that as it may, I shall not hesitate to make use of this manuscript if any bit seems worth salving; and perhaps the criticism is not worthless after all, for I do remember that when, some years later, a French writer produced an appreciation, his victim was amiable enough to tell me that it was a poor thing of which the best part was a paraphrase of what I had already published. Naturally I remember the compliment, but now, looking at it suspiciously, I cannot quite decide from which hand it comes.

As I was saying, that I should have been one of the first to sing the praises of Virginia Woolf is not surprising. I had known her since she was a girl of twenty, and in the years between my marriage to her sister in 1907 and her marriage to Leonard Woolf in 1912 I was to some extent her literary confidant. From earliest days I admired her reviews in *The Times Literary Supplement*, *The Cornhill* and *The Guardian*, and perhaps that was why she took me into her confidence and showed me short imaginative pieces few, if any, of which have been printed. Why should they have been? To me they were thrilling because they revealed—so I thought and thought rightly—in a person I cared for, genius; but to a coldly critical eye perhaps they would have seemed no more than a gifted girl practising. During these years we met regularly, once a week I dare say, to talk about writing generally and her writing in particular; with pleasure I remember that already I possessed sufficient sense of proportion to say nothing about mine. And yet we contrived to quarrel occasionally: we were both young. I call to mind some famous rows: and I have by me a picture post-card from Siena, written many years later, with an inky cross against a spot on the fortezza and beneath this legend—'Here Clive quarrelled with his sister-in-law'.

However, it is neither about our bookish talks nor yet about her books that I want to say my word, though doubtless I shall have said something about the latter before I have done. What I want to do is something much more difficult. I want to give an idea, an adumbration, of the most remarkable person I have known intimately. I cannot hope perfectly to succeed; the task is beyond my powers, and would, I fancy, be beyond the powers of any writer unless he were an artist possessing gifts comparable with those of his subject. Yet for a professional critic who has known and known well a genius—a genius who worked magic not only in art but in life; for such a critic, so fortunately placed, to despair of giving any account of the impression made on him, would be in my opinion poor-spirited. I will do my best. Two people I have known from whom emanated simply and unmistakably a sense of genius: the other is Picasso. With Picasso I have been acquainted for fifty years almost, and at one time I saw a good deal of him; but I do not pretend to have known him well. Picasso I would not attempt to describe, though later I may have some tales to tell about him. Nevertheless, had I never seen a picture by Picasso I should have been aware of his genius: I knew him well enough for that. Similarly, had I never read a book by Virginia I should have been aware of hers. It has been my fortune to be friends with a number of very clever people: Maynard Keynes, the cleverest man I ever met, Roger Fry, Lytton Strachey, Raymond Mortimer, Jean Cocteau. None of them cast the peculiar spell I am trying to characterise. The difference between these very clever people and the less clever, between Roger Fry and me for instance, was it seemed one of degree rather than kind. There was no reason in nature why I should not have been as bright as Roger, only I happened not to be. I can imagine myself as bright as Roger; I cannot imagine myself in the least like Virginia or Picasso. With Roger's understanding and mental processes mine were of a kind: I thought and reasoned and invented and arrived at conclusions as he did, only I thought and reasoned and invented less well. But Virginia and Picasso belonged to another order of beings; they were of a species distinct from the common; their mental processes were different from ours; they arrived at conclusions by ways to us unknown. Also those conclusions or comments or judgments or flights of fancy or witticisms, or little jokes even, were true or convincing or effective or delightful for reasons that are not the reasons of logic nor yet of our well tried common-sense. Their standards, too, were of their own creation: yet spontaneously we appraised by those standards, which for the moment we not only accepted but appropriated, whatever they chose to offer. Their conclusions were as satisfying as the conclusions of mathematics though reached by quite other roads; for though they might seem to have postulated that two and two made five their answers always came out right. All this is clumsy and perhaps beside the point. The point is that half an hour's conversation with Virginia sufficed to make one realise that she had genius.

I want in this attempt to describe Virginia to dispel certain false notions. One result of the publication of extracts from her diary (*A Writer's Diary*, Hogarth Press) has been to confirm an opinion already current, the opinion that Virginia's nature was harsh and unhappy. Nothing could be further from the truth. Yet, though the inference drawn from the published diaries is false it would be excusable had not the editor, Mr. Leonard Woolf, been at pains to put readers on their guard. On the very first page of his preface he writes: 'At the best and even un-expurgated, diaries give a distorted or one-sided por-trait of the writer, because, as Virginia Woolf her-self remarks somewhere in these diaries, one gets into the habit of recording one particular kind of mood —irritation or misery say—and of not writing one's diary when one is feeling the opposite. The portrait is therefore from the start unbalanced, and, if some-one then deliberately removes another character-istic, it may well become a mere caricature.'

Someone did remove another characteristic. The editor, himself, very properly cut out a number of passages which were much too personal, not to say libellous, to be published while the victims were alive.

Despite this warning, there are those who find confirmation in these diaries of what they wish to believe and retell the old tale—Virginia Woolf was gloomy and querulous; so I will add a few sentences to what her husband has said clearly enough. More often than not the diary was written in moments of agitation, depression or nervous irritation; also the published extracts are concerned almost entirely with her work, a subject about which she never felt calmly. Indeed, creating a work of art, as the diary shows, was for Virginia a cause, not only of moral but of physical exasperation—exasperation so intense that often it made per positively ill. I should not be surprised if some lively journalist had dubbed the book 'Screams from the torture-chamber', for truly much of it must have been written when the author felt much as one feels at the worst moments of tooth-ache. Even so, were the unpublished part (the published is not a twentieth of the whole) before the reader, it is certain that his idea of the writer would change completely. Of this unpublished part I know only scraps; and even these will not be printed for some years I surmise. Nor can I choose but rejoice; for amongst pages of gay and brilliant description will be found many disobliging comments on the sayings and doings and characters of her friends— of whom I was one. Wherefore here and now I should like to interpose a caution. Those comments and descriptions, those that I have read or heard read, though always lively and amusing are not always true.

Sooner or later Virginia's diaries and letters will be printed. They will make a number of fascinating volumes: books, like Byron's letters, to be read and re-read for sheer delight. In the midst of his delight let the reader remember, especially the reader who itches to compose histories and biographies, that the author's accounts of people and of their sayings and doings may be flights of her airy imagination. Well do I remember an evening when Leonard Woolf, reading aloud to a few old friends extracts from these diaries, stopped suddenly. 'I suspect', said I, 'you've come on a passage where she makes a bit too free with the frailties and absurdities of someone here present'. 'Yes', said he, 'but that's not why I broke off. I shall skip the next few pages because there's not a word of truth in them'.

That Virginia possessed the poet's, and dreamer's,

faculty of 'making Cables of Cobwebbes and Wildernesses of handsome Groves' will surprise no one who has read her books; what may surprise is that she should have employed this faculty not only in art but in life. I have gone so far as to conjecture—and it was going rather far I admit—that at times she saw life and to some extent experienced it as a novel or rather as a series of novels, in which anyone of her friends might find him or herself cast, all unawares, for a part. Yours might be a sympathetic rôle, and in that case all you said and did would be seen through roseate lenses, your banal comments would be transmuted to words of wisdom or subtle intuition, your ungainly gestures would acquire an air of dignity and significance. Sometimes, however—in my case generally—it was quite the other way. But for better or for worse one's character, conduct and conversation had to fit in to a picture which existed in the artist's imagination. To one's surprise, often to one's dismay, one found oneself the embodiment of a preconceived idea.

I felt so sure that there was something in my theory that I propounded it to one of Virginia's friends, from whom I heard a story to confirm my suspicions. This friend happened to be a lady, elegant and aristocratic to be sure, but unconventional to the verge of eccentricity. Her manners certainly were all that manners should be; but she was a rebel at heart, and her conversation and way of life would have shocked her mother profoundly and did shock her more sedate relations. No one could have been less like a leader of Victorian society. Nevertheless, in one of those marvellous romances which were a part of Virginia's everyday existence, that is what this wayward individual—Lady X shall we call her? —had to be: the typical leader of rather old-fashioned 'Society', exquisite and soignée (as she was) but also classically correct, smooth and sure of herself, running true to form in a world of dukes, ambassadors and orchids. To give a sharper point to this imaginary relationship—the friendship of a *grande dame* and a novelist—Virginia, who besides being one of the most beautiful was one of the best bred women of her age, cast herself in the rôle of a tough, uncouth, out-at-elbows Bohemian—of genius. And such was the spell she threw, such the cogency of her imagination, that many a time poor Lady X found herself, not only playing up to the rôle assigned to her, but positively accepting Virginia in the rôle she had allotted to herself. Am I not justified, then, in beseeching a vast posterity of enchanted readers to be on their guard?

To return for a moment to that silly caricature— Virginia the gloomy malcontent—let me say once and for all that she was about the gayest human being I have known and one of the most lovable. I was going to add 'besides being a genius'; but indeed these qualities were elements of her genius: in that sense she was all of a piece. I am not suggesting that she was faultless, or that those who have suspected her of being a little jealous on occasions or unwilling to 'brook a rival near the throne' were merely malevolent gossips. Only her jealousies and lapses of sympathy were of such a peculiar kind that it is difficult to understand them and easy to exaggerate. I do not pretend to understand them entirely, and so will give an example or two, leaving the reader to provide his own explanation. Someone said in her presence that it must be very tiring for her sister, a painter, to stand long hours at the easel. Virginia, outraged, I suppose, by the insinuation that her sister's occupation was in any way more exacting than her own, went out at once and bought a tall desk at which she insisted on standing to write. But this was when she was very young, and the very young are apt to be touchy. Surely she was guilty of excessive touchiness when she complained—a friend having told her I had said in a letter that she was looking well (she had been ill)—that 'Clive thinks I have become red and coarse'. It was a sort of jealousy, no doubt, that made her deprecate her friends pursuing the arts or professions which seemed in some way to put them in competition with herself. From time to time she would regret that Duncan Grant had not accepted a commission in the Black Watch—'I feel sure he would have been a remarkable soldier' (so do I). I believe she herself felt that she had gone a little far when she told me that Lytton Strachey should have been an Indian civil servant; but perhaps she was right when she persuaded Molly MacCarthy to write me a letter (to which I replied beginning 'Dearest Virginia') pointing out that critics were mere parasites on art and that my abilities (such as they were) would be much better employed at the bar. I think there was a sort of jealousy in all this, but I also think there was a sort, a very odd sort, of Victorianism. Sometimes it seemed to me that Virginia had inherited from her immediate ancestors more than their beauty and intelligence. Every good Victorian knew that a young man should have a sensible profession, something solid and secure, which would lead naturally to a comfortable old age and a fair provision for the children. In her head Virginia knew perfectly well that to give such advice to Lytton or Duncan was absurd; but Virginia, like the merest man, was not always guided by reason.

I said 'the merest man' because Virginia was, in her peculiar way, an ardent feminist. What is more, some of her injustices and wanton denigrations can be traced, I think, to female indignation. In political feminism—the Suffrage Movement—she was not much interested, though I do remember that once or twice she and I went to some obscure office where we licked up envelopes for the Adult Suffrage League. But, as you will have guessed, it was not in political action that her feminism expressed itself: indeed she made merciless fun of the flag-wagging fanaticism of her old friend Ethel Smythe. What she minded most, perhaps, was what she considered male advantages, and especially advantages in education. Readers of *A Room of One's Own* will remember an amusing, but none the less bitter, comparison of lunch in King's with dinner at Girton; and intelligent readers will have felt that the comparison is to be carried a great deal further. Also she resented the way in which men, as she thought, patronised women, especially women who were attempting to create works of art or succeed in what were once considered manly professions. Assuredly Virginia did not wish to be a man, or to be treated as a man: she wished to be treated as an equal—just possibly as a superior. Anyhow the least suspicion of condescension irritated her intensely and understandably. She grew angry and lashed out; and her blows fell, as often as not, on innocent noses. She could be monstrously, but delightfully, unfair; and witty blows below the belt sometimes leave nasty bruises. Neither male nor female can be wholly objective about *Three Guineas*; but for my part I feel sure it is her least admirable production.

Virginia's feminism was genuine and ardent, yet I do not think it played a great part in her life. Certainly the tantrums to which it gave rise were rare and transitory; and I will make bold, and bold it is, to say that hers was a happy nature. I know all about those fits of black despair; she had something to be desperate about, seeing that always hung over her the threat of collapse if she indulged too freely her ruling passion—the passion to create. Writing was her passion and her joy and her poison. Yet, I repeat, hers was a happy nature and she was happy. As for her gaiety—does this seem significant? My children, from the time they were old enough to enjoy anything beyond their animal satisfactions, enjoyed beyond anything a visit from Virginia. They looked forward to it as the greatest treat imaginable: 'Virginia's coming, what fun we shall have'. That is what they said and felt when they were children and went on saying and feeling to the end. And so said all of us. So said everyone who knew her. 'What fun we shall have' and what fun we did have. She might be divinely witty or outrageously fanciful; she might retail village gossip or tell stories of her London friends; always she was indescribably entertaining; always she enjoyed herself and we enjoyed her. 'Virginia's coming to tea': we knew it would be exciting, we knew that we were going to laugh and be surprised and made to feel that the temperature of life was several degrees higher than we had supposed.

I have not yet said what I want to say, I have not succeeded in giving an idea of Virginia's high spirits and lovable nature, so let me try another method. Barbara Bagenal was a girl of whom Virginia was fond; but Barbara Bagenal would be the last to claim that she was one of Virginia's closest friends. However, Barbara was down on her luck: she had been looking forward to a grand holiday, six weeks in Spain, and a day or two before she was to start she had been struck down by scarlet fever. That was a disaster with the misery of which Virginia could sympathise, and she showed her sympathy to some purpose. To her unhappy friend in hospital she wrote, and wrote precisely the sort of letters anyone in hospital would like to receive. The nurses insisted on burning most of them, but here is one that escaped.

Hogarth House. 24th June 1923

My dear Barbara,

'I should have written to you before, but I have had so many disasters lately from writing letters that nothing short of death or bankruptcy will in future draw one from me. I hope scarlet fever isn't about as bad as going bankrupt. I have often thought of you in your hospital,

as I take my way about the streets in comparative freedom. Yet I would have changed places with you last
Sunday fortnight, when Ottoline completely drew the
veils of illusion from me, and left me on Monday morning to face a world from which all heart, charity, kind-
ness and worth had vanished. How she does this, in 10
minutes, between 12 and 1, in the best spare bedroom,
with the scent of dried rose leaves about, and a little
powder falling on the floor, Heaven knows. Perhaps after
37 under-graduates, mostly the sons of Marquises, one's
physical life is reduced, and one receives impressions
merely from her drawl and crawl and smell which might
be harmless in the stir of normal sunlight. Only is the
sunlight ever normal at Garsington? No, I think even
the sky is done up in pale yellow silk, and certainly the
cabbages are scented. But this is all great rubbish. We've
had a desperate afternoon printing, and I'm more in
need of the love of my friends than you are. All the 14 pt.
quads have been dissed into the 12 pt. boxes! Proof taking has been made impossible; and Eliot's poem delayed
a whole week. I'm sure you'll see that this is much more
worth crying over than the pox and the fever and the
measles all in one.[1] Do you have horrid old gamps who
come and cheer you up? By which I mean tell you stories
about their past grandeur, and how they have come
down in the world, or they wouldn't be nursing the likes
of you—by which they mean that you haven't got silk
chemises. I could write you a whole page about their
talk, but refrain. Here is a quotation from a letter I've
just had from Roger[2], in Salamanca. "I was really rather
surprised to see Saxon Turner approach the table at
Segovia where I was seated with one Trend, a Cambridge musician; he approached the table in perfect
style with just a little guttural noise, a sort of burble,

[1]Mrs. Bagenal was suffering from scarlet-fever only.
[2]Roger Fry.

which expressed everything that the moment demanded, and sat down, and we went about very happily for some days. He became quite talkative. And really what a nice creature he is." So our poor old Saxon is moving among the living. He disappeared in such gloom, owing to your loss, that I've since thought of him as a kind of seagull wailing forlornly round the coast on windy nights. You won't be lacking in letters from him. And they will tell you every detail. London is spasmodically gay, that is to say I dine out in humble places and went to the opera one night, and one night to the Italian puppets, and one night to see Nessa,[1] and another to dine with Maynard.[2] Leonard is frightfully busy. We meet on the stairs oftener than anywhere, and I'm not sure that the glories of the *Nation*[3] are quite worth so much energy. Mrs. Joad is doing very well—much better to be honest than dear old Ralph, but then she is a daily worker, enthusiastic sanguine, and much impressed by small mercies.[4] If only she didn't scent herself, rather cheaply, I should have nothing to say against her. She is a character so entirely unlike my own that I can't help gaping in astonishment as we sit at lunch. Fancy playing tennis in Battersea Park! Fancy having a mother who lives at Harpenden! Fancy eating up all the fat, because it's good manners! Carrington insisted on meeting her. I don't think they received good impressions of each other.'

(I must omit a passage which contains scurrilous, and probably untrue, reflections on a person now alive).

[1]Vanessa Bell.
[2]Maynard Keynes.
[3]Leonard Woolf was at that time literary editor of *The Nation*.
[4]Mrs. Joad was working for the Hogarth Press, where she succeeded Ralph Partridge and Barbara Bagenal herself.

'Duncan was very severely treated by Simon Bussy in the *Nation*. Nevertheless he has sold almost every picture, I hear; and they say this will revive poor Roger's miseries about his own failure; but Roger, of course, is far the nicest human being of any of us, and will as usual be incomparably more generous than one could suspect Christ to be, should Christ return, and take to painting in the style of Cézanne at the age of 56. Clive, who has nothing Christlike about him, has had to give up eating tea, because, when Lady Lewis gave a party the other night and Rosenthal played Chopin, a waistcoat button burst and flew across the room with such impetuosity that the slow movement was entirely spoilt.[1] The humiliation, which would have killed you or me—the room was crowded with the élite of London—only brushed him slightly—he won't eat bread and butter any more; but his spirits are superb, and he says that life grows steadily more and more enchanting, the fatter one gets. Mr. Bernard Shaw almost agreed to review his book for the *Nation*;[2] and said so on a post card, but Clive is very touchy about post cards from Bernard Shaw and has never forgiven Carrington, nor ever will.'[3]

(With deep regret I omit a particularly entertain-

[1] I don't think it happened quite like that. For Rosenthal read Rubinstein, probably.

[2] Strange, if true; the only thing I published about that time was a little essay *On British Freedom*, it seems unlikely that Bernard Shaw would have heard of it.

[3] Carrington had sent me a card, purporting to come from Bernard Shaw and complaining of something I had said about him in print. I was taken in. Carrington and Logan Pearsall Smith were the hoaxers in chief of the age. Personally, I never cared for practical jokes and hoaxes; but when I described them as 'fools' wit' Pearsall Smith took it in bad part. May I add that Carrington and I remained fast friends to the day of her death?

ing paragraph which contains statements that may well be true but are certainly libellous).

'I hope you realise that though I am chattering like a pink and yellow cockatoo (do you remember Mrs. Brereton's poem, Pink and yellow, pink and yellow?) I'm a chastened raven underneath: I mean I am very much concerned at your miseries, which besides being in themselves odious, show a mean malignity on the part of Providence which makes me, for once, a Christian and a believer. If there was not a God, of course you would have gone to Spain with Saxon: as it is, there you are in bed at Maidstone. Our only alleviation of HIS afflictions is to send you our latest, *Talks with Tolstoi*—a very amusing book, even when it has passed through the furnace, which I suppose it must do, before reaching you.[1]

'Leonard is still trying to take proofs in the basement. I have cheered myself up by writing to you, so please don't say that I've plunged you into despair, as another invalid did the other day, when I cheered myself up by writing to her.

'Please get well, and come and see me. Barbara Chickybidiensis is one of those singular blooms which one never sees elsewhere, a rare and remarkable specimen.[2] I wish I could write an article for Outdoor Life about you, and get £50. £25 should then be yours. Love to Nick. Let me know how you are.

Yr. V.W.'

[1]No: it would have to pass through the furnace—if it passed through the furnace at all—after and not before reaching the invalid.

[2]Walking in the garden at Rodmell, Virginia had noticed a flower which struck her as not quite a common nasturtium. She enquired the name. Out came Barbara with 'Tropaeolum Canariensis'. So grand a name, delivered with such authority, by so small a creature, took Virginia's fancy, and she christened her flower-like little friend 'Barbara Chickybidiensis'.

That Virginia should have written such a letter to one who, as I have said, would not claim to have been of her nearest and dearest, will give some idea of her thoughtful and affectionate nature: the letter itself gives a taste of her gaiety, spirits and power of invention.

But of course it was in conversation that her gaiety poured out most abundantly. Her talk, as my friend Raymond Mortimer would say, was 'dazzling'. It was unlike any other I have heard, though at moments that of Jean Cocteau, at his best, has reminded me of it. To describe conversation is notoriously impossible, and to report it verbatim is not easy. I know it is supposed to be the secret of Boswell's success, but I have sometimes wondered whether Johnson did say exactly what Boswell makes him say. I, at any rate, cannot report conversations word for word: and when I have told the reader that the quality of Virginia's came in part from the apparent whimsicality and from the unexpectedness of her notions and comments, partly from a happy choice of words and constructions, hardly at all from the manner of delivery, but chiefly from sheer magic, I believe I shall not have brought him much nearer the heart of the mystery. The melancholy fact is that till her familiar correspondence has been published, even a vague idea of the fun and spirit of Virginia's talk can hardly be gained by those who did not know her. As the correspondence—or the best part of it—cannot yet be published, admirers must try to catch a taste of the delicious treat that was her company from passages such as this: '. . . To show how very little control of our possessions we have—

what an accidental affair this living is after all our civilization—let me just count over a few of the things lost in one lifetime, beginning, for that seems always the most mysterious of all losses—what cat would gnaw, what rat would nibble—three pale blue canisters of book-binding tools? Then there were the bird cages, the iron hoops, the steel skates, the Queen Anne coal-scuttle, the bagatelle board, the hand organ—all gone, and jewels too. Opals and emeralds, they lie about the roots of turnips. What a scraping paring affair it is to be sure! The wonder is that I've any clothes on my back, that I sit surrounded by solid furniture at this moment. Why, if one wants to compare life to anything, one must liken it to being blown through the Tube at fifty miles an hour—landing at the other end without a single hair pin in one's hair! Shot out at the feet of God entirely naked! Tumbling head over heels in the asphodel meadows like brown paper parcels pitched down a shoot in the post office!...'

This fragment from that enchanting soliloquy, *The Mark on the Wall*, may perhaps give a hint of what it was like when Virginia indulged in a flight of fancy, as she often did. Of her full length books I think *Orlando* gives the best idea of her with her elbows on the tea-table letting herself go. I am not sure that it is not my favourite of all her works, though of course I do not consider it the best. That, no doubt, is *The Waves*. Indeed, if I were writing as a critic, instead of what they call a 'fan', I should be inclined to say that *The Waves* and perhaps *To The Lighthouse* were the only perfect masterpieces she ever produced. To me *The Waves* seems perfect;

whereas I perceive that a stern critic could pick a hole or two in most of the others, and more than two in *Orlando*. Only, if he find fault with *Orlando*, he must find fault with *Tristram Shandy* too; and it seems a pity, should one have the luck to possess a sense of beauty and a sense of humour, to accept grudgingly either of these exquisite satisfactions.

Just now I pictured Virginia with her arms on the tea-table. The image came to mind naturally enough. Often I think of her in the dark dining-room at Rodmell or at the round painted table of Charleston, childishly revelling in cakes and honey, enjoying them as she enjoyed the accompanying gossip and nonsense, herself the life and inspiration of the party. The 'tea-table' I said, and so saying unintentionally gave myself an opportunity of putting a stop to one of the most preposterous lies that ever came into circulation. A year or so before the war I found myself in Paris sitting at dinner next an attractive young French woman who turned out to be a passionate admirer of the novels of my sister-in-law. Naturally she questioned me, and naturally I supplied information of the banal kind one does supply on such occasions. Amongst other things I told her that the artist was handicapped by the constant menace of a nervous disorder which, when it attacked her, made any sort of intellectual effort impossible and reduced her to a state of agitated misery. 'Ah yes', said my pretty neighbour, 'Ah yes', and said it with a sorrowful, meaning look which was not meant to escape me. Quite at a loss, I exclaimed,

'What on earth are you driving at?' 'Well', she said, 'Well, everybody knows—whisky'.[1]

As my old nurse would have said, you could have knocked me down with a feather. As soon as I had recovered my balance I explained that normally Virginia never touched alcohol of any sort, for she did not much like it. Indeed it was a standing joke —every set of intimate friends has its standing jokes —that 'Clive always makes me drunk', by which she meant that when she dined with me I would, if I could, cajole her into drinking a glass of wine or half a glass at any rate. The fact that this grotesque fabrication appears to have been accepted as true by people who certainly wished Virginia no ill, should be, I suppose, a warning to biographers. I have a fondness for gossip and am perhaps too willing to give mongers the benefit of a doubt. But this bit positively shocks me, not because I object to people getting drunk, but because the notion of Virginia as a dipsomaniac is absurd beyond the limits of absurdity. So I trust that anyone who does me the honour of reading this paragraph, and happens to hear the lie repeated, will do truth the honour of contradicting it flatly.

In my attempts to sketch the characters of other old friends I have adopted the classic method of recalling particular sayings and doings which seemed

[1] As I have admitted that I cannot report a conversation verbatim, let me further admit that the only words faithfully reproduced here are 'Ah' and 'Whisky': we were talking French.

notably characteristic and pinning them down; but with Virginia that method will not do. Everything she said or did, the way she propounded a theory or uttered an exclamation, the way she walked or dressed or did her hair (not very securely), the way she cut a cake (not very neatly), or laughed or sneezed, was peculiar and characteristic. Admirers in search of a memorable image will find my account inadequate, and admirers will be right. As I have sadly admitted more than once, until all the letters and diaries have been published they cannot hope to possess anything like a portrait of the artist: all they can do is to seek her in her books, and these, though of course expressive, do not reveal the whole nor perhaps the most fascinating part. Still, when they have enjoyed her art for its own sake, some are sure to begin wondering just how much of the artist it really does reveal. I will help them in their quest if I can. And now it seems to me possible that by extracting certain passages from that essay—written with Virginia just round the corner and in the knowledge that it would be read and criticised by her—by extracting passages, or elaborating them, I may put the curious on a profitable track.

I then said that what made Virginia Woolf's books read queerly was that they had at once the air of high fantasticality and blazing realism. This, I think, is true, and the explanation may be that, though she is externalising a vision and not making a map of life, the vision is anything but visionary in the vulgar sense of the word. Her world is not a dream world; she sees, and sees acutely, what the reviewer in a hurry calls 'the real world'—the world of Miss Austen and George Eliot, of *Madame Bovary* and *War and Peace*. It is a perfectly comprehensible world in which no one has the least difficulty in believing: only she sees it in her own way. She sees life more purely than most of us see it; and that may mean that sometimes she sees it less passionately. Sometimes she seems to be watching through a cool sheet of glass two lovers (say) on a bench in the park: she will know well enough what they are saying and know (not feel) what they are feeling; she will miss not one subtle, betraying gesture; she will be aware of the romance, but she will not share the romantic emotions. In the strictest sense of the word she is a seer. More often than not her creative impulses spring from her sense of a scene. And this pure, this almost painterlike, vision sets her far apart from the common or garden realists, her contemporaries.

Of course literary art cannot be much like painting; for it is out of words that writers must create the forms that are to clothe their visions, and words carry a significance altogether different from the significance of lines and colours. Virginia, as a matter of fact, had a genuine and highly personal liking for pictures.[1] But her sense of visual values revealed itself most clearly, and characteristically, in a feeling for textures and the relations of textures. She would pick up a feather in the fields and set it in an appropriate wine-glass against a piece of stuff carelessly pinned to the wall, with the taste and 'rightness' of a Klee, if not a Picasso. But that, though I

[1]Herself, she occasionally made drawings, which are said to show considerable talent. They accompanied letters which I have not seen.

H

hope it may be of interest to some of her admirers, is beside my immediate point. What I am trying to say is that her vision, and superficially her style, may remind anyone, as it reminded the French critic, M. Abel Chevalley, of the French Impressionists. Her vision may remind us of their passion for the beauty of life, loved for its own sake, of their abhorence of sentimentality, and of their reputed inhumanity; while technically her style may remind incorrigible seekers after analogy of little touches and divisions of tone. We are familiar with the way in which Renoir and Monet proclaim their sense of a garden blazing in the sun. It is something that comes to them in colours and shapes, and in shapes and colours must be rendered. Now see how an artist in words deals with a like experience.

'. . . How hot it was! So hot that even the thrush chose to hop, like a mechanical bird, in the shadow of the flowers, with long pauses between one movement and the next; instead of rambling vaguely the white butterflies danced one above another, making with their white shifting flakes the outline of a shattered marble column above the tallest flowers; the glass roofs of the palm house shone as if a whole market full of shiny green umbrellas had opened in the sun; and in the drone of the aeroplane the voice of the summer sky murmured its fierce soul. Yellow and black, pink and snow white, shapes of all these colours, men, women, and children were spotted for a second upon the horizon, and then, seeing the breadth of yellow that lay upon the grass, they wavered and sought shade beneath the trees, dissolving like drops of water in the yellow and green atmosphere, staining it faintly with red and blue. It seemed as if all gross and heavy bodies had sunk down in the heat motionless and lay huddled upon the ground, but their voices went wavering from them as if they were flames lolling from the thick waxen bodies of candles. Voices. Yes, voices. Wordless voices, breaking the silence suddenly with such depth of contentment, such passion of desire, or, in the voices of children, such freshness of surprise; breaking the silence? But there was no silence; all the time the motor omnibuses were turning their wheels and changing their gear; like a vast nest of Chinese boxes, all of wrought steel turning ceaselessly one within another, the city murmured; on the top of which the voices cried aloud and the petals of myriads of flowers flashed their colours into the air.'

No one, I suppose, will deny the beauty of that. No one ever has denied that Virginia Woolf chooses and uses words beautifully. But her style is sometimes accused, injuriously, of being 'cultivated' and 'intellectual'—obviously such criticism would be inapplicable here—especially by people who themselves are not particularly well off for either culture or intellect. Cultivated it is, in the sense that it reveals a finely educated mind on terms of easy acquaintance with the finest minds of other ages; and perhaps it is cultivated also in the sense that to enjoy it a reader must himself be pretty well educated. No doubt it makes unobtrusive reference to and recalls associations with things of which the unlettered dream not. Intellectual? Yes, it is intellectual in that it makes demands on the reader's understanding. However, it is not difficult in the way that the style of philosophers and philosophic writers must be difficult, since it is for visions and states of mind and not for logical processes and abstract reasoning that this author finds verbal equivalents. She has no call to chop logic so her prose can be musical and coloured; also as she has no taste for violence it can be cool. Though colder far, the lyrical passages in her novels are nearer to the last act of Figaro, to that music which gives an etherial sense of a summer night's romance, than to the second act of Tristan which gives . . . Well, the over-sexed will appreciate the art of Virginia Woolf hardly; the fundamentally stupid never.

Yet it cannot be denied that reasonable people have complained—'Virginia Woolf's novels make stiff reading'. Generally, I think, any trouble they may have in following the movements of her mind is caused not by eccentricity of expression but by the complexity of what is being expressed. For just as there are subtleties of thought which a philosopher cannot, with the best will in the world, make as plain as a police-court statement, so there are subtleties of feeling which an artist cannot express as simply as Tennyson defined his attitude to Lady Clara Vere de Vere. Those who in moments of vexation call her writing unintelligible are, I suspect, unless merely thick-witted, making the mistake that was made by the more enlightened opponents of Impressionism. They are seeking noon at twilight. They are puzzled by a technique which juxtaposes active tones, and omits transitions which have no other function than to provide what modern painters and Virginia Woolf and perhaps the majority of serious contemporary writers hold to be unnecessary bridges. For my part, I shall not deny that I am a little old for jumping, or that in literature I love a bridge, be it merely a plank. My infirmities, however, are unimportant. The important thing is that Virginia Woolf's words and phrases are chosen deliberately, with exquisite and absolute precision, to match her meaning, and that they form a whole which perfectly envelops her vision.

I have tried, by recalling memories and touching on her art, to give what I confessed at the outset would be no more than an adumbration of Virginia Woolf. It now seems to me, re-reading what I have written, that I have failed—and this is perhaps my worst omission—to convey a sense of her magic— for Virginia was a magician in life as well as in art. Can I mend matters, I wonder, by calling to mind at this eleventh hour something that happened many years ago when, after one of her recurrent collapses, she was sent by her doctor to a convalescent home kept by an amiable and commonplace woman called, shall we say, Miss Smith? Although Virginia was ill and intellectually and emotionally below normal her magic within a day or two had done its work; Miss Smith was transformed. Nothing like this had happened to her before; suddenly life, which she had found drab and dreary, had become thrilling and precious. Every moment counted; for everything seemed exciting or amusing. Positively the poor woman started, on the sly, to struggle with the poets; but soon discovered that she had no need for books, her own life, coloured by the presence and idle talk of her patient, having grown poetical. For the first, and I dare say last, time she was living intensely. As she tried to explain to me one afternoon when Virginia, whom I was visiting, was tak-

ing a rest, for the first time in her life she felt of
consequence to herself; she was aware of her own
existence, she said, and all the trivial things that
made up that existence had significance too. The
magician had cast her spell, and Miss Smith, like
any poet, was seeing the world in a grain of sand.
Whether the spell endured after the magician had
departed I do not know; I should think it unlikely.
But during a month or six weeks 'the world' for Miss
Smith was 'so full of a number of things' that she,
the matron of a nursing home, 'was as happy as' a
queen: and I dare say a good deal happier.

This transformation seemed miraculous because
the transformed was what is called 'a very ordinary
woman'. But the effect of Virginia on her closest
friends was not different in kind. I remember spending some dark, uneasy, winter days during the first
war in the depth of the country with Lytton Strachey. After lunch, as we watched the rain pour down
and premature darkness roll up, he said, in his
searching, personal way, 'Loves apart, whom would
you most like to see coming up the drive?' I hesi-
tated a moment, and he supplied the answer: 'Virginia of course'. Be sure her magic would have
worked on him as it had worked on Miss Smith.

VII

ENCOUNTERS WITH T. S. ELIOT

IT would be better, of course, if he were to record his encounters with me, for in that way students, besides enjoying a bit of prose by our best living poet, might learn the exact truth: the author of *Mr. Apollinax* is surely one to remember dates and details. So far as I can remember, it was in the summer of 1916 that first we met. Bertrand Russell asked me to look out for a man called 'Eliot' who had just come, or was just coming, to England, and had been his best pupil at Harvard: he may have said 'My only good pupil', but if so, doubtless he exaggerated as philosophers will. Eliot came to dinner at 46 Gordon Square, where I was living with Maynard Keynes; however, I was alone that night, and so after dinner the poet and I sat in my room at the top of the house and talked about books. I was not sure that he altogether liked my enthusiasm for Mérimée's stories and Horace Walpole's letters; but for my part I liked him so much that I determined, there and then, to make him acquainted with some of my friends. Soon afterwards I introduced him to Roger Fry and Virginia Woolf, both of whom were to play parts in later encounters.

Virginia liked Tom from the first and appreciated his poetry: also she teased him. Roger was excited and enthusiastic, and, as usual when excited, constructive. He it was who urged Eliot to elucidate the text of *The Waste Land* with explanatory notes. Eliot met him half-way: he supplied notes, but whether they are explanatory is for others to decide. Between Virginia and myself somehow the poet became a sort of 'family joke': it is not easy to say why. To some people the combination of human frailties with supernatural powers will always appear preposterous, which is, I suppose, a roundabout way of saying that a poet is an oddity. To us at any rate this mixture, talent, in its rarest form, combined with studied primness of manner and speech, seemed deliciously comic. Besides, Virginia was a born and infectious mocker. I would receive a post-card, for in those happy days (the early 'twenties' maybe) there was no telephone at Charleston, my summer refuge: 'Come to lunch on Sunday. Tom is coming, and, what is more, is coming with a four-piece suit'. This came from Rodmell, five or six miles away, where Leonard Woolf still lives, where Eliot was a frequent visitor, and whence frequently he was brought to Charleston for a meal. One of these meals, a dinner-party, he will hardly have forgotten.

He will remember it not so much for what was said as for what was done. We had been sent a brace of grouse. My wife, who takes my opinion on sporting matters and on no others, enquired whether this would be enough for a party of eight. I said it would not, and that a bird between two was a fair allowance. She thinks she may have confused this estimate with something I had once said about snipe—two a mouth. Anyhow more grouse were ordered, and, when the soup-plates had been cleared away, entered three platters supporting sixteen birds—ten on table and six on the sideboard. Even the inventor of Sweeney appeared to think this unusual. The evening was not to end, however, without its contribution to scholarship; for somebody wondered whether anything was known of Mrs. Porter and her daughter beyond the fact that they wash their feet in soda water. 'These characters are known', said the master, 'only from an Ayrian camp-fire song of which one other line has been preserved:

And so they oughter.

Of such pieces, epic or didatic', he continued, 'most have been lost, wholly or in part, in the mists of antiquity; but I recall one that is generally admitted to be complete:

Some say the Dutch ain't no style, ain't no style,
But they have all the while, all the while.'

And this reminds me of a poem I once wrote, on T. S. Eliot, in French, and sent to Virginia on the back of a post-card. It is unlikely to have been saved: it was called *Sur le tombeau de Tom*.

I am getting a little out of date. If I met Eliot in 1916, it must have been in '17 that I went to Garsington for an Easter party taking with me some ten or dozen copies of the last, and perhaps the first, publication of the Egoist Press, 'The Love Song of J. Alfred Prufrock'. Anyone with a taste for research can fix the date, for the book, or brochure rather, had just appeared and I distributed my copies hot from the press like so many Good Friday buns. Who were the recipients? Our host and hostess, Philip and Lady Ottoline Morell, of course. Mrs. St. John Hutchinson, Katherine Mansfield, Aldous Huxley, Middleton Murry, Lytton Strachey perhaps, and, I think, Gertler. Were there others? Maria Balthus for instance (later Mrs. Aldous Huxley). I cannot tell: but of this I am sure, it was Katherine Mansfield who read the poem aloud. As you may suppose, it caused a stir, much discussion, some perplexity. I wonder how many of us have kept our copies. Mine I have stowed in some secret place where I cannot now lay hands on it. Already it must be worth a deal of money; for, not only is it the first edition of a fine poem by a fine poet, of one of his earliest works too, but, unless I mistake, the brochure itself is bound in a trashy yellow jacket and is badly printed on bad paper. Misprints, if I remember right, and letters turned upside-down are discoverable. In a word, it is the sort of thing for which bibliophiles give hundreds. But though it must be amongst my most valuable mislaid possessions, I esteem it less than certain envelopes addressed, after the manner of Mallarmé, in verse, and addressed to me. Of these I own several, which, by taking pains, I could bring to light; but happily I may spare myself a dusty search since only the other morning arrived what will serve to give a taste of my correspondent's mettle.

> *O stalwart SUSSEX postman, who is*
> *Delivering the post from LEWES,*
> *Cycle apace to CHARLESTON, FIRLE,*
> *While knitting at your plain and purl,*

ENCOUNTERS WITH T. S. ELIOT

Deliver there to good CLIVE BELL,
(You know the man, you know him well,
He plays the virginals and spinet),
This note—there's almost nothing in it.

For the benefit of the author I may say that this
pleasantry gave satisfaction to the postman invoked.
He considered it 'clever'. He was not quite sure
about the 'spinet', but knew that I was fond of a bit
of shooting: it was not true about the 'virginals' he
hoped.

At Sunday evening performances, especially those
given by the Phœnix Society, I used to admire Mr.
Eliot's faultless dress, white waistcoat and all:
whether at an evening party, or in the country (you
will remember the 'four piece suit') or in the city,
always the poet made himself inconspicuous by the
appropriateness of his costume.

Flowed up the hill and down King William Street
To where Saint Mary Woolnoth kept the hours
With a dead sound on the final stroke of nine.
There I saw one I knew, and stopped him, crying: 'Stetson!'

I might have cried 'Tom: cry you mercy, I took you
for a banker'. And a banker he was in these early
days; at least he worked in a bank. How characteristic! And how wise! Instead of doing as most young
poets of promise do, eking out a living with journal-
ism, which slacks the sacred strings, thus too often
belying the promise, Eliot stuck to his desk—in King
William Street or thereabouts, and found time of an
evening to say all that he deemed worth saying. I

doubt whether in his poems—his plays are another thing—he has written a slovenly or an otiose line. He has kept his honour as bright as La Bruyère kept his.

If T. S. Eliot were not a famous poet, he would be known as a remarkably clever man. This cleverness comes out delightfully in conversation, and it came out rather unexpectedly one night at a birthday party given in her riverside house by Mrs. St. John Hutchinson. She had invited, so she said, the ten cleverest men in London to meet the ten most beautiful women: those who were not invited are not obliged to consider her judgment infallible. After supper we pulled crackers; and Lady Diana Cooper, having surreptitiously collected the riddles in which, along with caps and whistles, crackers used to abound, mounted a chair and announced that she would now put our wits to the test. She read the riddles aloud, and almost before the question was propounded pat came the answer from two of the guests: Maynard Keynes and T. S. Eliot. You might have supposed that a certain sedate primness of speech, inherited maybe from a line of New England ancestors, would have put Eliot at a disadvantage. It did. Luckily, Maynard Keynes, when excited, sometimes developed a slight stutter. He stuttered ever so little on this occasion but he stuttered sufficiently; the handicaps were equal, and the two cleverest of the clever ran neck and neck all the way. It is only fair to add that Aldous Huxley might have come in a better third had not righteous indignation provoked by the imbecility of the conundrums, in some measure balked the stride of his lofty intellect.

ENCOUNTERS WITH T. S. ELIOT

If in this little chapter—a mere hand wave and doffing of the hat to an old and illustrious friend—I have done nothing to explain the nature of his gift, I shall not apologize. Anyone who cares enough about poetry to read tittle-tattle about a poet needs no help from a tattler.

VIII

BLOOMSBURY

THERE is mystery in the word, and money too perhaps. Or is it merely for fun that grave historians and pompous leader-writers no less than the riff-raff of Fleet Street and Portland Place chatter about the thing? 'The thing', I say, because that is the least committal substantive I can think of, and it is not always clear whether what the chatterers are chattering about is a point of view, a period, a gang of conspirators or an infectious disease. Beyond meaning something nasty, what do they mean by 'Bloomsbury'? Assuming, as seems reasonable, that they all have in mind, amongst other things, a gang or group or clique (for without human beings you cannot well have a point of view or a doctrine, and even an epidemic needs 'carriers'), I invite them to name the men and women of whom this gang or group or clique was composed. Who were the members of Bloomsbury? Let them give the names: then they may be able to tell us what were the tastes and opinions held in common by and peculiar to the people to whom these names belong, what, in fact, is or was the 'Bloomsbury doctrine'.[1]

[1] *The Times Literary Supplement* (20 August 1954) published a long review of a book the name of which escapes me. This review, or essay rather, was entitled 'The air of Bloomsbury'; and is by far the most intelligent and penetrating piece that has been written on the subject. There were errors of fact to be

But we must not ask too much—and it is much to think clearly and state one's thoughts perspicuously —of columnists and broadcasters, so to *The Times Literary Supplement* and a Fellow of All Souls I turn. The *Supplement* has before now castigated Bloomsbury in reviews and even in a leading article; while only the other day I caught one of the most prominent fellows of the glorious foundation writing in *The Times* of 'Bloomsbury historians'. From such high courts we may expect clear judgments. I implore the *Supplement*, I implore Mr. Rowse, to give categorical answers to a couple of straight questions: (*a*) Who are or were the members of Bloomsbury? (*b*) For what do they, or did they, stand?

I have been stigmatized as 'Bloomsbury' myself, and the epithet has been applied freely to most of those who are, or were—for many are dead—my intimate friends, so, if it be true that something that can fairly be called 'the Bloomsbury group' did exist, presumably I am entitled to an opinion as to who were the members and what were their thoughts and feelings. Of course I am aware that people born in recent years and distant lands hold opinions clean contrary to mine. By all means let them enjoy a Bloomsbury of their own invention; only, should

sure, errors there must be in an appreciation by someone who is not himself a part of the society described, by someone who was neither an eye nor an ear witness. But the essay, admirably written, reveals a remarkable power of understanding complex characters and peculiar points of view. It has value much beyond that of most ephemeral, or rather hebdomadal, criticism. And it is to be hoped that it will soon be published in easily accessible and durable form.

they chance to write on the subject, let them state clearly whom and what they are writing about. Otherwise historians unborn will flounder in a sea of doubt. Knowing that 'Bloomsbury' was the curse of a decade or two in the twentieth century, but unable to infer from a mass of woolly evidence who precisely were the malefactors and what precisely was the thing, some will be sure that it was a religious heresy, a political deviation or a conspiracy, while others, less confident, may suspect it was no more than a peculiar vice.

So, having appealed to the highest authorities for simple answers to simple questions, I now repeat my request to the smaller fry. Let everyone have his or her notion of 'Bloomsbury'; but let everyone who uses the name in public speech or writing do his or her best to say exactly what he or she intends by it. Thus, even should it turn out that in fact there never was such a thing, the word might come to have significance independent of the facts and acquire value as a label. I dare say Plato would have been at a loss to discover the connection between his philosophy and the epithet 'platonic' as used by lady-novelists and reviewers in the nineteenth and twentieth centuries; nevertheless in refined conversation the word now has a recognised meaning. 'Bloomsbury' may yet come to signify something definite, though as yet few people, so far as I can make out, understand by it anything more precise than 'the sort of thing we all dislike'. Wherefore I repeat, let publicists and broadcasters be explicit. That is my modest request: which made, I will give what help I can by telling all I know.

BLOOMSBURY

The name was first applied to a set of friends by Lady MacCarthy—Mrs. Desmond MacCarthy as she then was—in a letter: she calls them 'the Bloomsberries'. The term, as she used it, had a purely topographical import; and the letter, which doubtless could be found at the bottom of one of five or six tin boxes, must have been written in 1910 or 1911. But the story begins earlier. It begins, as I have recorded in an earlier chapter, in October 1899 when five freshmen went up to Trinity—Cambridge, of course—and suddenly becoming intimate, as freshmen will, founded a society as freshmen almost invariably do. It was a 'reading society' which met in my rooms in the New Court on Saturdays at midnight, and here are the names of the five original members: Lytton Strachey, Sydney-Turner, Leonard Woolf, Thoby Stephen, Clive Bell.[1] After he had gone down, and after the death of his father, Thoby Stephen lived at 46 Gordon Square, Bloomsbury, with his brother Adrian and his two sisters Vanessa (later Vanessa Bell) and Virginia (later Virginia Woolf). These two beautiful, gifted and completely independent young women, with a house of their own, became the centre of a circle of which Thoby's Cambridge friends were what perhaps I may call the spokes. And when, in 1907, the elder married, the circle was not broken but enlarged; for Virginia, with her surviving brother Adrian, took a house in nearby Fitzroy Square: thus, instead of one *salon*—if that be the word—there were two *salons*. If ever

---

[1] I maintain that A. J. Robertson was also an original member, but he disclaims the honour—or dishonour.

such an entity as 'Bloomsbury' existed, these sisters, with their houses in Gordon and Fitzroy Squares, were at the heart of it. But did such an entity exist?

All one can say truthfully is this. A dozen friends —I will try to name them presently—between 1904 and 1914 saw a great deal of each other. They differed widely, as I shall tell, in opinions, tastes and preoccupations. But they liked, though they sharply criticised, each other, and they liked being together. I suppose one might say they were 'in sympathy'. Can a dozen individuals so loosely connected be called a group? It is not for me to decide. Anyhow the first World War disintegrated this group, if group it were, and when the friends came together again inevitably things had changed. Old friends brought with them new and younger acquaintances. Differences of opinion and taste, always wide, became wider. Close relationships with people quite outside the old circle sprang up. Sympathy remained. But whatever cohesion there may have been among those who saw so much of each other in Gordon Square and Fitzroy Square, among Lady Mac-Carthy's 'Bloomsberries' that is, by 1918 had been lost. That was the end of 'old Bloomsbury'.

Now I will try to name these friends. There were the surviving members of the Midnight Society. Thoby Stephen had died in the late autumn of 1906: Leonard Woolf was in Ceylon between 1904 and 1911: remained in Bloomsbury Lytton Strachey (who, in fact, lived in Hampstead), Saxon Sydney-Turner, Clive Bell. There were the two ladies. Add to these Duncan Grant, Roger Fry, Maynard Keynes, H. T. J. Norton and perhaps Gerald Shove, and I believe you will have completed the list of those of the elder generation who have been called 'Bloomsbury'. Certainly Desmond and Molly MacCarthy and Morgan Forster were close and affectionate friends, but I doubt whether any one of them has yet been branded with the fatal name. So much for the old gang.

As I have said, after the war a few men of a younger generation became intimate with most of us. I will do my best to name these, too; but as the new association was even looser than the old, the classification will be even less precise. First and foremost come David Garnett and Francis Birrell, both of whom we—by 'we' I mean the old Bloomsberries —had known and liked before 1914. Immediately after the war, by a stroke of good luck, I made the acquaintance of Raymond Mortimer;[1] and about the same time Lytton Strachey, lecturing at Oxford, met Ralph Partridge. I do not know who discovered Stephen Tomlin: but I remember well how Keynes brought Sebastian Sprott and F. L. Lucas from Cambridge to stay at a house in Sussex shared by him with my wife, myself and Duncan Grant. I think it may have been through Francis Birrell that we came to know a brilliant girl from Newnham, Frances Marshall (later Mrs. Ralph Partridge).

Now whether all or most of the people I have named are the people publicists have in mind when they speak of 'Bloomsbury' is not clear. In fact that

[1]Raymond Mortimer reminds me that, after the first war, he was brought to 46 Gordon Square by Aldous Huxley. That was our first meeting.

is one of the questions I am asking. But from words let fall in broadcasts and articles I infer a tendency to lump together the two generations and call the lump 'Bloomsbury'. We can be sure of nothing till the journalists and broadcasters and the high authorities too have favoured us with their lists. I have given mine; and so doing have given what help I can and set a good example. I have named the friends who were intimate before 1914 and have added the names of those, or at any rate most of those, who became friends of *all* these friends later. Naturally, with time and space at their familiar task, the bonds of sympathy loosened—though I think they seldom snapped—and so the friends of 'the twenties' were even less like a group than the friends of the pre-war period. That, as I have said, has not prevented some critics lumping them all together, and calling the combination or compound, which it seems exhaled a mephitic influence over the twenties, 'Bloomsbury'. It is impossible, I repeat, to know whom, precisely, they have in mind; but, assuming their list to be something like mine, again I put the question: What had these friends in common that was peculiar to these friends?

Not much, I believe you will agree, if you will be so kind as to read my chapter to the end. For beyond mutual liking they had precious little in common, and in mutual liking there is nothing peculiar. Yes, they did like each other; also they shared a taste for discussion in pursuit of truth and a contempt for conventional ways of thinking and feeling—contempt for conventional morals if you will. Does it not strike you that as much could be said of many collections of young or youngish people in many ages and many lands? For my part, I find nothing distinctive here. Ah, say the pundits, but there was G. E. Moore the Cambridge philosopher; Moore was the all-pervading, the binding influence; 'Moorism' is the peculiarity the Bloomsberries have in common. I should think there was G. E. Moore; also the influence of his *Principia Ethica* on some of us was immense—on some but not on all, nor perhaps on most. Four of us certainly were freed by Moore from the spell of an ugly doctrine in which we had been reared: he delivered us from Utilitarianism. What is more, you can discover easily enough traces of Moorist ethics in the writings of Strachey and Keynes and, I suppose, in mine. But not all these friends were Moorists. Roger Fry, for instance, whose authority was quite as great as that of Lytton Strachey was definitely anti-Moorist. So, in a later generation, was Frances Marshall who, beside being a beauty and an accomplished ballroom dancer, was a philosopher. Assuredly Raymond Mortimer, Ralph Partridge and Stephen Tomlin—all three Oxford men—were not devout believers in *Principia Ethica*; while F. L. Lucas, who in those 'twenties' may well have heard himself called 'Bloomsbury', at that time called himself a Hedonist. I doubt whether either of the Miss Stephens gave much thought to the all important distinction between 'Good on the whole' and 'Good as a whole'. Also it must be remembered that Bertrand Russell, though no one has ever called him 'Bloomsbury', appeared to be a friend and was certainly an influence.

Lytton Strachey, I have agreed, was a Moorist. Of him I have written at some length elsewhere and have said that, being a great character, amongst very young men he was inevitably a power. But at Cambridge, and later among his cronies in London, his influence was literary for the most part. He inclined our undergraduate taste away from contemporary realism towards the Elizabethans and the eighteenth century. But when, about 1910, Roger Fry and I became fascinated by what was being written in France he did not share our enthusiasm. Quite the contrary: and as for contemporary painting, Lytton, who had a liking, a literary liking, for the visual arts, thought that we were downright silly about Matisse and Picasso, and on occasions said so.[1] It begins to look—does it not?—as though this thing called 'Bloomsbury' was not precisely homogeneous. Maynard Keynes, whose effect on economic theory was, I understand, immense, bore no sway whatever amongst his friends in the West Central district. They liked him for his cleverness, his wit, the extraordinary ingenuity with which he defended what they often considered absurd opinions, and his affectionate nature. They disliked other things. He had very little natural feeling for the arts; though he learnt to write admirably lucid prose, and, under the spell of Duncan Grant, cultivated a taste for pictures and made an interesting collection. Said Lytton

[1]Well do I remember Lytton drawing me aside and saying: 'Cannot you or Vanessa persuade Duncan to make beautiful pictures instead of these coagulations of distressing oddments?' Duncan Grant at that time was much under the influence of the Post-Impressionists and had been touched by Cubism even.

once: 'What's wrong with Pozzo'—a pet name for Maynard which Maynard particularly disliked—'is that he has no æsthetic sense'. Perhaps Lytton was unjust; but with perfect justice he might have said the same of Norton. On the other hand, Pozzo and Norton might have said of some of their dearest friends that what was wrong with them was that they were incapable of wrestling with abstractions. You see we were not so much alike after all.

I have done my best to name those people who certainly were friends and of whom some at any rate have often been called 'Bloomsbury'. I have suggested that the people in my list held few, if any, opinions and preferences in common which were not held by hundreds of their intelligent contemporaries: I emphasise the words 'in common'. Wherefore, if my list be correct, it would seem to follow that there can be no such thing as 'the Bloomsbury doctrine' or 'the Bloomsbury point of view'. But is my list correct? It should be. And yet I cannot help wondering sometimes whether the journalists and broadcasters who write and talk about Bloomsbury have not in mind some totally different set of people. There are critics and expositors, for instance that leader-writer in *The Times Literary Supplement*, who describe Bloomsbury as a little gang or clique which despises all that is old and venerable and extols to the skies, without discrimination, the latest thing whatever that thing may be—the latest in art or letters or politics or morals. Also, according to this school of critics, the writers of Bloomsbury delight in a private and cryptic language, unintelligible to the common reader, while mocking at whatever is clear and comprehen-

sible. Now who are these crabbed and wilfully obscure writers who despise all that is old? Surely not
those reputed pillars of Bloomsbury, Lytton Strachey, Roger Fry, Maynard Keynes, David Garnett?
I beseech the *Supplement* to give us the names.[1]

There are other critics, of whom I know as little
as they appear to know of the reputed pillars of
Bloomsbury, who hold a clean contrary opinion. I
write from hearsay; but I am told there are brisk
young fellows, authorities on the 'twenties', whose
distressing accents are sometimes heard on the wireless by those who can stand that sort of thing, who
explain that in 'the twenties' there still existed in
England a gang or group which for years had devoted itself to stifling, or trying to stifle, at birth
every vital movement that came to life. Oddly
enough this gang, too, goes by the name of Bloomsbury. Now who can these baby-killers have been?
Obviously not Roger Fry who introduced the modern movement in French painting to the British
public, nor Maynard Keynes, who, I understand,
revolutionised economics. Nor does it seem likely that
the critics are thinking of Lytton Strachey who, far
from being reactionary, went out of his way to help
the cause of Women's Suffrage when that cause was
reckoned a dangerous fad, or of Leonard Woolf who
was a Fabian long before British socialism had become what the Americans call a racket. Whom can
these castigators of 'Bloomsbury' have in mind?

[1] A week or so after this leading article appeared Mr. Oliver
Strachey made the same request, and received from the *Supplement* (31st July 1948) what I can only consider a disingenuous
reply.

Clearly not Virginia Woolf who invented what amounts almost to a new prose form; nor, I hope, certain critics who, long before 1920, had appreciated and defended the then disconcerting works of Picasso and T. S. Eliot.

Once more I cry aloud: Who were the members of Bloomsbury? For what did they stand? In the interests of history, if common decency means nothing to them, I beseech the Bloomsbury-baiters to answer my questions; for unless they speak out and speak quickly social historians will have to make what they can of wildly conflicting fancies and statements which contradict known facts. Thus, disheartened by the impossibility of discovering opinions and tastes common and peculiar to those people who by one authority or another have been described as 'Bloomsbury', the more acute may well be led to surmise that Bloomsbury was neither a chapel nor a clique but merely a collection of individuals each with his or her own views and likings. When to this perplexity is added the discovery that no two witnesses agree on a definition of the 'Bloomsbury doctrine', historians are bound to wonder whether there ever was such a thing. At last they may come to doubt whether 'Bloomsbury' ever existed. And did it?

IX

PARIS 1904

EVERY biographer knows that the undergraduate years are, or were, the most important, the most 'formative' to use an up-to-date expression, in a man's life—that is of a man who enjoyed the fortune of having been educated at Oxford or Cambridge. To me came the luck of a second formative period, the luck of a year in Paris when I was between twenty-two and twenty-three. In this chapter I shall try to recall my first acquaintance with Paris, commemorating in the attempt two friends, Morrice and O'Conor.[1] Of French friends I shall say little or nothing, for at that time I had none—no real friends, I mean. In another place I will speak of Copeau and Vildrac, Derain and Segonzac, Cocteau, Georges Duthuit, Matisse and Picasso, whom I came to know later and may, I hope, call 'old friends' though I may not call them intimate. But with Morrice and O'Conor for a time I was intimate; and as at that time I was young they left deep impressions on my tender mind. Of those later friends, French friends it would be silly and impudent to attempt an appreciation such as I have attempted in the case of Lytton Strachey, Roger Fry or Virginia Woolf, and when you come to read what I have to say about

[1]Unlike those who have written about him O'Conor spelt his name with one 'n'. I have letters to prove it.

them—if, indeed you read so far—you will find I have nothing better to offer than a handful of anecdotes and memories. But of Morrice and O'Conor, though I was in daily company with them for a little while only, I can write more knowingly. They played as influential a part in my life as any of my Cambridge contemporaries; inevitably, seeing that they and Gerald Kelly were the first painters I knew really well. For, at the time I was meeting these three men every day almost I had seen but little of that admirable paintress who was to become my wife, and could profit little by occasional encounters with second-rate French artists for the very good reason that I understood their language imperfectly and spoke it abominably. Wherefore to these three English-speaking painters I owe a vast debt of gratitude. Unluckily for me some four months after I first met him Gerald Kelly disappeared from our quarter and hid himself in the wilds of Montmartre. It was left to Morrice and O'Conor to continue my education.

I took my Bachelor's degree in June 1902, and though, to my tutor's annoyance and George Trevelyan's amusement, I obtained only a second, my college—Trinity—thought proper to offer me the Earl of Derby studentship. Accordingly I set myself to collect material for a dissertation on British policy at the Congress of Verona, and divided the academic year—October 1902 to August 1903—between Cambridge and the Record Office. In the late summer of that year I went most unwillingly with my father to shoot at animals in British Columbia. When I returned to England in November I realised that if ever I was to make anything of my dissertation I must continue my studies, not in the Record Office, but in the *Archives*. So to Paris I went in January 1904; and having been honoured by the personal inspection and presumably the approval of one of M. Delcassé's underlings I was permitted to begin my researches. They did not go far: I visited the *archives* thrice I believe. Nevertheless, the year 1904 was one of the most profitable of my life. Instead of going to the *archives* I went daily to the Louvre.

Like any other well meaning English boy I took lodgings in a *Pension* with a view to acquiring a better knowledge of French than my expensive education had provided. The Pension was kept by one Madame B——, a youngish widow, tolerably handsome and as hard as nails. We got on together well enough. Her house stood in a street which I can no longer find, though it is said to exist, la rue Bouquet-de-Longchamps, just behind the Trocadéro. There I began to stammer and half understand French, thanks partly to Madame and partly to a captain of the Colonial army, home from Indo-China, on long leave I suppose: I forget his name. Luckily he was one of those people who delight in giving information. Madame had designs on him I fancied. He may have been her lover, but I doubt it. He ate but did not sleep in her house. Anyhow, during the weeks I spent under Madame B——'s roof—weeks in which as I have said I acquired a smattering of French, as well as some knowledge of the paintings in the Louvre and of the streets on the north bank of the Seine—all I knew of Parisian 'night-life' came from occasional outings with this captain. I remember going with him, over-dressed in our swallow-tails and white ties, to see Sarah Bernhardt in *La Sorcière*—a shocking bad play I feel sure; and I remember how disappointing I found as much of it as I could understand. The captain was even more disappointed because he was on the look out for '*les jolies femmes et les belles toilettes*', and he saw little of either amongst the dumpy, *endimanchées* bourgeoises who were swallowing tepid white coffee and sandwiches in the foyer. The captain was a dull companion and the Pension a dull place—good for acquiring the rudiments of French though—and the Trocadéro quarter was not my quarter at all; nevertheless there I might have stayed for the rest of the year had I not come to Paris with a letter from E. S. P. Haynes to a young painter called Kelly. Probably it was not till the end of February or early March, not till I was beginning to feel at home in Paris, that I ventured to forward this letter, but a few days later I was knocking at a studio door in the rue Campagne-Première, a *cul de sac*, a warren of studios, just off the Boulevard Montparnasse.

Kelly, who had come to Paris in 1901, was a few years my senior; but, having spent three at Cambridge (Trinity Hall) he was a very young painter still. Also he was a painter of promise; and it is my belief that had he known how 'to feed on the advancing hour', had he about this time or a little later flung himself neck and crop into the contemporary movement, he might have found that nourishment for his talent which Spain and Java—so it seems to me—just failed to provide. In my opinion he has not fulfilled his promise: in my opinion, I say, because I do not suppose for a moment that Sir Gerald Kelly, P.P.R.A., considers himself a failure. Nor perhaps is he; for my part, I believe he is at the moment under-rated. I have seen good things by him in odd places—a surgeon's consulting room for instance—and I believe I could make a selection from his work which would surprise those critics who treat him as a nonentity. One thing is certain, he is about the best president the Royal Academy has given itself since Sir Joshua Reynolds. He has raised that foundation from the depths of public contempt to respectability if not honour. Anyhow in 1904 Kelly was an artist of promise: he was also a man of wit, culture and ideas, far better educated and more alert than the majority of his companions in the quarter, and I think it was partly because he enjoyed meeting someone with whom he could talk books and a little—a very little—philosophy that he took a fancy to me. You may wonder why he did not prefer to talk about these things with the French. I wonder too. As for me, during these first months in Montparnasse I was not sure enough of my hold on the subtleties of the language to butt into cultivated conversations—flirting with models and shop-girls was about as far as I dared go; but Kelly, like most of those who dined at the *Chat Blanc*, spoke French—or so it seemed to me at the time—fluently and correctly. When I consider how seldom during my solitary sojourns in Paris—and such sojourns have been frequent during a period of fifty years— how seldom I find myself speaking English, I am puzzled by the persistence with which these fluently

French-speaking English and American artists of the quarter for the most part kept themselves to themselves. Of course when the company was international they did speak French and spoke it easily; but then the conversation was apt to be trivial. Seemingly they reserved their graver and subtler thoughts for expression in their native tongue. Some of them had French mistresses—kept mistresses; but very few had French friends. They did not take part in the intellectual life of Paris. There must be some explanation. Maybe I shall hit on it presently. Meanwhile I take note that not long ago, in June 1947 to be exact, I observed that my friend Matthew Smith, who, since he has spent years in France doubtless speaks French easily, seemed to be seeking out English-speaking companions. This suggests that the tradition persists but does nothing to explain it.

Kelly, I say, took kindly to me because he needed a companion a little younger than himself with whom he could discuss matters, other than painting, in which he took an interest. But I do not suppose that the friendship would have ripened as it did —too quickly perhaps—had he not discovered to his surprise that this Earl of Derby student, this mugger up of dates and writer of dissertations, cared passionately for pictures, especially for those of the Impressionists, and appeared to know something about them. Had he not acquired, before coming to Paris, lithographs by Lautrec, and since his arrival had he not bought—for five francs—an etching by Renoir? That, I surmise, was what rendered me worthy of being taken to dine at the *Chat Blanc*, and afterwards to drink at the *Café de Versailles*. The first evening turned my head. When, after two more such evenings, Kelly suggested that I should leave my respectable *Pension* and take a room in the quarter I hardly knew whether I was standing on my heels or on that head. I trumped up an excuse for leaving the useful Madame B—— and her genteel neighbourhood, and some time in April found myself installed in the Hôtel de la Haute Loire, an *hôtel meublé*, at the angle of the boulevard Montparnasse and the boulevard Raspail. (The ground floor subsequently became Batty. What is it now? I don't know). In those days the boulevard Raspail ended in the boulevard Montparnasse: not until some years later was it driven down to the long unlovely rue de Rennes. Also in those days Montparnasse was not the centre of night-life it became later. There was no *Rotonde*, no *Select*, no *Bal nègre*, no *Boule blanche*, though the scrubby little café on which I looked from my bedroom window was called *Le Dôme*. Montmartre was still the artists' quarter: Montparnasse was a dingy suburb enlivened by English and American painters. To give you an idea of its isolation I may say that a visit to Montmartre—a visit some of us made from time to time—was matter for planning. One would walk across the Luxembourg gardens and lunch perhaps in a delightful little café—*Le Café Fleurus*—on the corner of the eponymous street, behind a flowery grill, looking on to the gardens. That was the first step: it brought one close to the Odéon, whence started every half hour a famous omnibus drawn by three greys abreast—Odéon–Clichy. And so, seated on the Impérial, one crossed Paris in an hour or less and finally climbed on foot to the Place du Tertre to have a drink before knocking at the door of some friendly studio. Having gone so far one stayed to dine; and every now and then O'Conor, Morrice and I would meet by appointment in Arnold Bennett's flat and take him to a *triperie*.

That was a great treat for Arnold Bennett, so we thought at the *Chat Blanc*. (What the *Chat Blanc* was I hope to explain in time). We were giving Bennett a taste of real Parisien life; so we thought, and upon my word I believe he thought so too. For Arnold Bennett, about 1904, was an insignificant little man and ridiculous to boot. Unless I mistake he was writing the 'Savoir Vivre Papers' for 'T.P.'s Weekly', and had written one or two trifling and ninetyish novels: above all he was learning French and he took longer about it than anyone has ever taken before or since. There we found him sitting in his little gimcrack apartment—I forget in which street, possibly la rue Fontaine—amidst his Empire upholstery from Waring and Gillow, with a concise French dictionary on the table, Familiar Quotations, *Whitaker's Almanack* and Morley's monographs on Voltaire and the Encyclopædists—these he admired hugely. He was the boy from Staffordshire who was making good, and in his bowler hat and reach-me-downs he looked the part. He was at once pleased with himself and ashamed:

> 'One of the low on whom assurance sits
> Like a silk-hat on a Bradford millionaire.'

We rather liked him, but we thought nothing of his writing. I do not think much of it now.

The Hôtel de la Haute Loire, in which I had a comparatively spacious bedroom and a minute *cabinet de travail*, lay midway between the two centres of Parnassian life—the *Café de Versailles* and the *Closerie des Lilas*. At the west end of what I may call our high street—the boulevard—stood the restaurant Lavenue—and what to us was more important its adjunct, Le Petit Lavenue; there, at the west end, stood also the Café de Versailles facing the Montparnasse railway-station oddly perched on what looked like a band-stand. Between the station and Lavenue there was just room for the entrance to the rue d'Odessa; and in the rue d'Odessa flourished the all-important *Chat Blanc*. A quarter of a mile or so away at the east end of the boulevard were the Bal Bullier and that most delightful of cafés (now smartened and ruined) La closerie des Lilas. This, as everyone knows, was a house of fame and literary repair; where Paul Fort and his colleagues of *Vers et Prose* held session; where later I was to hear Moréas declaim his 'Stances'; where was pointed out to me André Gide.

It was fifteen or sixteen years later that I came to know Gide: Copeau brought us together. But may I, taking advantage of the licence traditionally granted to rambling old memoir-writers, may I recount here and now the rather surprising episode which was my acquaintance with him. I feel pretty sure it was in the late autumn of 1919 that Copeau made us acquainted; and the acquaintance, as you will see, must have come to its unfortunate end before I abandoned the beautiful Hôtel Voltaire on the *quai* for the gloomy but highly convenient and less noisy recesses of the Hôtel de Londres. That more or less fixes the date for start and finish—the end of '19 to the summer of '22 or thereabouts. To show you how amiable Gide made himself I need give one instance only. I had invited him to meet an English lady at lunch chez Foyot—I remember being slightly pained when he watered the particularly good Burgundy I had ordered in his honour—and at coffee time he said he would like to commemorate the occasion by giving this charming lady an unpublished poem by Valéry which he thought would please her. It was a pretty, gallant little thing which, Gide supposed, would never be published. I am not sure he did not write it on a paper fan: the summer was hot, and in those days restaurants were apt to provide fans in hot weather. Anyhow, he wrote it out in his exquisite hand: I wonder whether the honoured recipient has it still. Some time later he and I lunched together at the Voltaire in the Place de l'Odéon, and Gide brought with him an extremely handsome and intelligent youth—let us call him 'Henri'. This youth had been reading a book of mine, with the greatest interest he said, and had noted points he would like to discuss. Of course I was flattered. 'Come to lunch with me one day next week', I said, 'and we will have it out'. 'It must be a Thursday or a Sunday', said 'Henri'—*jours de sortie*—which proves that he was still a student. 'Next Thursday', said I.

Next Thursday morning I was sitting in my untidy bedroom writing an article for *The New Republic* when who should be announced but 'Monsieur Gide'. We sat and talked a while, and then I said—

'I must wash and dress now for at one I am lunching, as you may remember, with "Henri".' 'En effet, en effet', said Gide, 'nous pourrions déjeuner ensemble—tous les trois'. We did, and needless to say there was no æsthetic discussion between 'Henri' and myself. But from that day Gide refused to speak to me. What is more, it took my friends in Paris some seven or eight years to persuade him that, given my abnormal normality, the intentions he attributed to me were out of the question. He was convinced at last, so my friends told me; but only once after that unlucky day did I hold converse with the master. I was dining alone, and probably reading *Le Temps*, in my habitual restaurant *Lafond* at the corner of la rue des Saints Pères: in came Gide with a party—mostly women and children it seemed to me: I believe they were going to the circus. He crossed to my table and said—I should like to have a word with you before we leave; shall I join you presently for a cup of coffee? Gide had something definite to say, he had a question to ask. 'Why does Aldous Huxley refer to me as a "faux grand écrivain"? he demanded; adding traditionally 'I have never done him any harm'. I could not say; but we passed the five minutes he had to spare well enough, speaking ill of Aldous presumably. Later I asked Aldous whether he had said anything of the sort. Yes, he had—some twenty years earlier in a magazine, possibly an undergraduate magazine. But Gide had the eyes of a lynx and the memory of an elephant.

Let me return to the Boulevard Montparnasse. Next door, or almost, to Les Lilas was an *Etablissement de Bains*, standing in a small garden, which, to me, was a place of some importance, seeing that in my hotel was neither bath-room nor hip-bath even. That was normal in 1904. A year and a half later, when I was living in St. Symphorien, a hamlet just across the river from Tours, the only way of coming at a bath was either to walk into the town or have a bath sent out to the hamlet.[1] As a rule I walked: but once, having fallen sick and been brought to convalescence by le docteur Pigeon—the youngest doctor in France according to himself—aided by a groaning table of drugs, I sent for a bath. Out came the water in a cylindrical boiler, with a smoking brazier hanging under it, drawn by a horse and accompanied by two stout *hommes d'équipe*. A long deep trough was borne into my room and the steaming water in cans; when I had returned to bed the water was withdrawn through the window by means of a pipe and the trough was carried coffinwise downstairs. Years later I recounted this surprising experience, as it seemed to me, to Othon Friescz, who assured me that it was not surprising at all. Indeed, he remembered that when he was a student, about the turn of the century, and inhabited the attic of a house—in Paris mark you!—wherein dwelt a lovely and promising young actress—he remembered, said he, that the young beauty had a bath sent in twice a week, and that when she was clean the spacious and scented tub was removed to the landing. Here, said he, as often as not it remained a while till the *hommes d'équipe* returned from lunch;

---

[1] It is now a large and flourishing suburb with an excellent restaurant.

and occasionally the under-washed and perhaps slightly amorous *rapin* would seize this opporunity and take a quick plunge. That at all events is what Friescz told me; but in story-telling, as in lapidary inscription, 'a man is not on oath'.

I was speaking—rather a long time ago I fear—of the *Chat Blanc* in the rue d'Odessa. There an upstairs room was reserved for an undefined group of artists, their friends, models and mistresses. Anyone might bring a friend whom he judged would be generally acceptable; and these friends became members, so to speak of the club. Mistakes were made sometimes. The only big-wig who came—and he came very rarely and to lunch only—was Rodin. I got into a scrape with him later for touching the drapery on a lay-figure in his studio. He paid me out too; for when I went with Thoby Stephen and O'Conor to offer incense one snowy *jour de l'an* he sent word that he was at home only to his 'amis les plus intimes'. I don't blame him. On the two or three occasions that I saw the great man at the *Chat Blanc* he was gracious enough. We all admired and fled him; for in conversation with us, his inferiors, he was tedious and unexpectedly pompous. Also he stank. His famous model Thérèse, to the splendour of whose forms the Hôtel Biron bears abundant witness, was a more regular and welcome attendant. So was Bonnat, not precisely a big-wig but an old painter whose connoisseurship we all respected: the collection he bequeathed to Bayonne proves how right we were. Two French artists pretty often to be found at dinner-time in our upper room were Ulmann,[1] a timid Whistlerian whose mistress had been a governess in Poland and never let one forget it, and Scott of *Illustration*. And then there was Madame Irma. So long as the Luxembourg gallery remained open, though stript of the Impressionists it was one of the most depressing spots in Europe, I entered from time to time to glance at a painting by Dugardier; for there, walking on the sands in a boater was his enchanting model, Irma. I wonder what has become of that picture. Probably it is in the depths of the *dépôt national*. Besides being a beauty, Irma was a wit, and a *très brave fille* to boot. A passionate cyclist, she was the first woman wearing bloomers with whom I ever sat down to dine; also she was the first I ever saw pick up her plate and lick it clean. I learnt much from Irma.

Three decorated Americans frequented the *Chat Blanc*: the painter, Alexander Harrison, who flaunted the rosette of glory, the sculptors Brooks and Bartlet, merely beribboned. We saw and heard a good deal of Stanlaus, a young and successful American illustrator; also of the Englishmen, Howard, Kite and Thompson. Thompson, whose paintings I never saw, was also a good pianist and a lady-killer; Howard (called Pompey) was mixed up somehow with the legation at the Hague; Kite—a follower of Lavery—was a joke, and Irma called him 'Joseph'.

I set down these recollections of the *Chat Blanc* some years ago, and have since read a delightful essay by Somerset Maugham in which he gives his

[1] So his name is written by Mr. Donald Buchanan in his biography of J. W. Morrice. I had imagined it was Huilman.

account of the goings on in that upper room. He frequented it, he says, in 1904; but I cannot help thinking it must have been earlier, unless it were in the first three months of 1904 only. From April to Christmas of that year I dined there about five nights a week, except during the holiday months of August and September, and I never met Maugham though often I heard him spoken of. It is impossible that I should have forgotten it had I met him: Somerset Maugham is not a man to be forgotten or overlooked. Besides, I remember distinctly the excitement of coming to know him some years later in London. He says that Anrold Bennett dined in the restaurant once a week. In my day he never came there, though, as I have said, Morrice, O'Conor and I occasionally called for him in his flat. (Let me, by the way, seize this opportunity of recommending to anyone who has not read it Maugham's description of that flat, which he thinks may have been in the rue de Calais). But what convinces me that he is describing a *Chat Blanc* of an epoch earlier than mine is his account of the intellectual atmosphere that prevailed there. 'We discussed', he says, 'every subject under the sun, generally with heat', and recalls a discussion of Heredia's poetry into which were dragged the names of Degas, Mallarmé and Charles-Louis Philippe. In my day the intellectual atmosphere had deteriorated sadly, partly perhaps owing to the disappearance of Maugham. Heated discussions on literary subjects were seldom if ever heard. Only a smutty story or a denigration of Whistler by O'Conor was likely to raise the temperature a little above normal. The name of Hérédia might have been pronounced;

Degas was mentioned from time to time no doubt
—but not nearly so often as Whistler, Conder or
Puvis de Chavannes. No one, I think, but O'Conor
would have read Mallarmé. Both he and I might
have read *Marie Donadieu*, but we should have
known better than to speak of so recondite a work
to Stanlaus or Root.[1]

The 'regulars' of whom I saw most were Kelly,

[1] I have called attention elsewhere to a trivial mistake made
by Mr. Buchanan, and I may add that Somerset Maugham
also spells O'Conor with two 'n's. But to tell the truth I here
mention Mr. Buchanan's slip only to give myself an excuse for
again mentioning his book and calling attention to an admirable account of Arnold Bennett at the *Chat Blanc* contributed
to that book by Sir Gerald Kelly:

'I used to dine once a fortnight', says Sir Gerald, 'or once
a week with Bennett, alternately in Montmartre where he
lived, or in Montparnasse, where I lived. We were both
poor and, of course, each paid on the principle of a Dutch
treat.

Thus I had introduced Bennett to the *Chat Blanc*. He liked
Morrice very much. I believe I am right in remembering that
Morrice didn't very much care for him. At that time Bennett
was rather a figure of fun. His teeth stuck out through his upper
lip. He talked through his nose, and with the most appalling
accent. He had, through nervousness or from vanity, the most
overbearing, showy manner, and mentally and physically his
favourite attitude was with his thumbs in the armholes of his
waistcoat. Everything comic amused Morrice and he could
find comedy when a great many people could not, but after a
little while (if I remember aright) he found Bennett a little
overwhelming. I think all my acquaintances at the *Chat Blanc*
found Bennett rather overwhelming, though he only came once
a fortnight or once a month. I have a kind of recollection that
I was criticised for having brought him.' (*James Wilson Morrice—A Biography*, by Donald W. Buchanan. The Ryerson
Press, Toronto).

O'Conor and Morrice. During the summer months of 1904 Kelly was, I suppose, my closest friend. As for his influence, I may say that, in imitation of one of his sartorial flights of fancy, I sported on occasions a Lavallière. Yes, I have been seen by people now alive wearing a Lavallière bow at the *Café de Régence*. Kelly worked hard during the day, and I do not think we ever went picture-gazing together. But we talked pictures, and from him I learnt something about the technique of oil-painting and lithography. Mostly, however, our conversation was bookish; and I have surmised that it was because Kelly found in me someone with whom he could gossip endlessly about English literature that he saw much of me. He read aloud admirably—he had won the Winchester Reading Prize at Cambridge—and sitting in his studio looking out on that long, romantic stable-yard—for that is what the rue Campagne-Première is—sometimes before dinner, more often late at night by the light of a *lampe à pétrole*, he would neatly articulate a poem by Browning or a chapter of Meredith—two of his favourites—part of an Elizabethan play, a bit of Milton or Keats, or an essay by Oscar Wilde—another favourite. It was sitting here in the late dusk of a long June evening that we came in for a little comedy that entertained us considerably and sticks in my memory. Opposite Kelly's studio lodged in a small apartment a young paintress whose name I must not reveal—let us call her Helen Vavasour—of no great talent but endowed with appreciable beauty and a turn for high-falutin that fairly took one's breath away. Well, on this calm evening, appeared beneath her window a young

American painter, an occasional diner at the *Chat Blanc*, who perhaps had been absent for a day or two since he carried a Gladstone bag. There, in the gloaming, he stood beneath her window and called discreetly, 'Helen', 'Helen'. Beautiful, tall and tragic Miss Vavasour came to the window, and this is what she said: 'I have eliminated the material'. Someone had been putting ideas into the girl's head, we surmised. Could it have been Kelly's brother-in-law Alaister Crowley? It doesn't sound like him. But one never knows: besides, Miss Vavasour may have got it wrong. Anyhow, there in the dusk stood the young American: I can see him now in his white flannel trousers—yes, white flannel trousers—his bag dropped beside him, bewildered, staring. And this, picking up his bag, is what he said: 'I suppose that means I can't sleep here tonight'. Off he marched.

I knew Crowley: he came sometimes to the *Chat Blanc*, and sometimes took his *apéritif* at the *Versailles*. Sitting there one evening and turning to me, he exclaimed suddenly: 'I will take you to dine at Paillard's'—Paillard was at that time one of the most fashionable and expensive restaurants in Paris. I was by no means dressed for the occasion, and this I pointed out. In fact I was extremely shabby, not to say grubby; so, as you may suppose, I took my seat at the table, to which we were shown by an elegant waiter, in a state of some uneasiness. Crowley disappeared for a moment and returned observing— 'It will be all right, I have told the *maître d'hôtel* that you are a Russian prince'. When we left there was a dispute about the bill. After dinner Crowley offered to take me 'where he would not take everyone'.

In fact we went to the *Caveau des Innocents* and *L'Ange Gabriel* in *Les Halles*, two underground eating-houses which remained open all night for the porters and market-gardeners. I forget into which of the two we ventured first: whichever it may have been, as it was about ten o'clock, of course it was empty. To be exact, there were a couple of soldiers playing dominoes in a corner. 'They always keep soldiers on duty here', whispered Crowley, 'they dare not do less'. As I had drunk brandy enough already, and as it was obviously my turn to play host, I called for a bottle of white wine. 'Ah, you shouldn't have done that', said Crowley, 'they will see that we have money'. After living dangerously in one establishment for about twenty minutes, we moved to the other. Here a young gentleman did approach our table and asked permission to take our portraits. He made two heavy pencil drawings which we took away with us, and gave him in return two francs and a glass of wine. After that, we felt that honour was satisfied and thankfully returned to the *Versailles* for a glass of beer. Crowley seemed to feel that we had looked pretty steadily into the jaws of death. I could not share his emotions, but of course he may have been right.

The Canadian, J. W. Morrice, an excellent painter whose work, though fairly well known, is in my opinion still insufficiently admired, would be described, I suppose, as an Impressionist of the second generation. As a youth he had studied in a Canadian university and even taken a degree—at least I think he had: also he retained a taste for, and a taste in, the 'humanities' as he liked to call them. It goes

without saying that his father wished him to enter
the family business, which I have heard was highly
profitable, or to become a lawyer. Instead he crossed
to England, half hoping he once told me—but he
was drunk at the time—to become a professional
musician. He was an accomplished flautist, when he
could keep his breath, and a passionate lover of
music: I believe he told me that he had played in
the Hallé orchestra, but I do not think that can have
been true. How he came to France and under whom
he studied I do not know. He had been a friend of
Conder and an acquaintance of Lautrec; the influence of Harpignies, Manet, Monet and Whistler is
discoverable in his early and middle periods. He
must have known Bonnard and Vuillard, though he
never spoke of them to me; and I dare say he and
O'Conor were the only *habitués* of the *Chat Blanc* who
in 1904 had even heard of either of them, which
gives you the measure of our provincialism. Morrice
would have been about forty when I met him, and
all through his life his art continued to develop. As
early as 1911 or '12 he fell in with Matisse at Tan-
giers; and during the 1914–18 war saw much of
him. The art of Matisse had considerable influence
on that of Morrice. This is much to the credit of the
latter; for he was already a mature and fairly successful painter in another style. He preserved an
open mind and sensibility, and was capable of profit-
ing by new methods and a younger man's vision.
But essentially he was a solitary artist. He had a
great deal of character, which is by no means the
same thing as having a strong character: he *was* a
character. Had he been more often sober, probably

he would have painted more and larger pictures, but I doubt whether he would have painted better. Many of his things are sketchy, I admit; but all are charming and personal.

Morrice was of the *Chat Blanc–Versailles* connection, but its cosy parochialism did not satisfy him. He liked knocking about Paris and sometimes he took me with him. From Morrice I learnt to enjoy Paris: to be sure I was a willing pupil. Also from Morrice I learnt more about pictures; and it was he who later advised me to look at Matisse. Here I cannot be sure of dates; but certainly it was before I had the surprise of being shown, in Florence, and at Mr. Berenson's table of all places, photographs of some drawing by that master. I think I was in Florence in the spring of 1908; I know that I had the honour of lunching with Berenson, and I remember that we did not lunch at *I Tatti*. Now I know why: *I Tatti* was undergoing alterations. Well do I remember admiring those photographs and maybe expressing my admiration tactlessly; for what I did not know at that time was that with the great critic the subject of Matisse was one to be handled gingerly. Some months earlier he had decided that a room at *I Tatti* should be decorated by a modern artist: he would give the *fauves* a chance of showing whether there was anything in them. This bold resolution boiled down to a choice between Matisse and Piot. The great man plumped for Piot; and at the moment I was going into indiscreet raptures over Matisse the Piot decorations were being concealed. After they had been executed and paid for, Mr.

Berenson discovered that he did not like them. *I Tatti* was uninhabitable.[1]

The Paris to which Morrice introduced me, the Paris of 1904, was still the Paris of the Impressionists. It was a city of horse-omnibuses and yellow *fiacres* and drivers with shiny white 'toppers'; of craftsmen working, with a 'hand' or two in their own shops; of good living and low prices. It was a Paris without a 'metro'; but those yellow fiacres would take you almost anywhere it seemed for a franc and a half: indeed, late at night, even though you were as far afield as Montmartre, you had only to spot a cab with a green light—which meant that the horse's stable was in Montparnasse—and the driver could generally be argued into taking you home for a franc, plus of course the standard tip of five sous. The *Café de la Paix* and the restaurant behind it were still the favourite cosmopolitan haunts. Morrice would say—'Let us go and drink a Pernod at the *Café de la Paix* and look at the *rastas* as O'Conor calls them'. In 1904 the echoes of the Dreyfus case were still audible; the Congregations were being

[1]The story goes—I do not vouch for it—that Berenson, having commissioned Piot to decorate his library (I think) went abroad. On his return, seeing what had been done, he gave orders that it should be obliterated. He had forgotten that the Italian government, with his approval—sanction should I say?—had made a law that no wall-paintings in Italy were to be destroyed. But Piot had not forgotten. Accordingly, Piot's decorations could not be destroyed but had to be concealed beneath boards and canvas at considerable expense. If the story be true, they must still be on the walls or ceiling at *I Tatti*, unseen but intact.

harried, or thought they were; I dare say Emile Combes was *président du conseil*.

This Paris was still full of little music-halls and *cafés chantants*; Morrice delighted in such places— places where waiters circulated taking orders for drinks during the performance, places where one kept one's drink in front of one on a ledge provided for the purpose. Even at the *Concert Rouge*, where a capable quartet played exclusively classical music, this pleasing habit obtained: *cerises au cognac* was the thing to order there. The *Concert Rouge* was a favourite with Morrice; it stood opposite Foyot and so was on his way from the *quais* to the *Versailles*. But he liked almost as well, though in a different way perhaps, *La Cigale*, a little Montmartrois music-hall decorated by Willette: it was there I feel almost sure I first heard Jeanne Granier. Morrice was one of those fortunate people who enjoy beauty as they enjoy wine; both were for him necessities and he was not too difficult about the vintage. Beauty he found everywhere; in streets and cafés and *zincs* (the word 'bar' was still a stranger in the French language) in shop-windows and railway-stations, in the circus and on penny-steamers. There is nothing surprising about that; all these were recognised beauty-spots in Impressionist days. But Morrice could take pleasure in an evening at the Opéra or the Opéra-Comique, and that was quite irregular. True to his generation he had a taste for Pernod, and was exceptional only in his taste for several in succession; but he would not drink them anywhere. He had the knack of discovering sympathetic *endroits*: sometimes it would be a large and superficially garish café, sometimes a

discreet retreat. He might give you rendezvous for
six o'clock at what then seemed a vast new *brasserie*
on a populous *place* or in an almost undiscoverable
Louis-Philippe box in a bye-street. Always the place
had character; and always Morrice enjoyed it for
what it was worth and made his companion enjoy
it too. One of his favourite words was 'gusto', used,
as he would observe with gusto, in the sense in which
Hazlitt used it. He read little, but he enjoyed what
he read. He read newspapers and he read poetry;
and he enjoyed both. He enjoyed his round, merry
mistress, Léa, but he kept her in her place, that is,
on the fringe of his life. He enjoyed her meridional
accent, and especially her impulsive habit of using
the meridional expletive, '*Pardi*'.

As I have said, Morrice moved about Paris more
than did most of the frequenters of the *Chat Blanc*.
Topographically he was not of the quarter but of
the centre rather, inhabiting the quai des Grands
Augustins—number 35 if I remember right. Certainly his studio—a not very big room over-looking
the river—must have been close to *La Pérouse*, for on
the rare occasions when he settled down to work in
the morning he would have the *plat du jour* and a
bottle of wine sent up from the restaurant. The normal Parnassien—the hideous word Montparnois had
not yet been coined—was unbelievably regional in
those days. Only serious business or planned and
premeditated pleasure took him far out of a terri-
tory bounded by the boulevard St. Michel, the rue
Denfert-Rochereau, the cemetery, the Avenue du
Maine, the rue de Sèvres and the boulevard St. Ger-
main. The Gaité Montparnasse and the Bobino were

his theatres; and when he had money to burn he would take a girl to dine at the Taverne du Panthéon—dinner at the Panthéon (without wine) might cost as much as five or six francs a head. An excited party might press on to Bullier, a hundred yards or so up the boulevard, but would hardly have pushed down across the bridges. Morrice, however, would go anywhere that was not too smart. It was he who took me to the tart-parade at Olympia and to dine at the Horse Shoe, an English House near the Gare du Nord, familiar to students of Huysmans. Morrice had an 'emphatic gusto', to borrow one of his favourite expressions, for a vaguely Dickensian England and Scotch Whisky—especially if they could be had in Paris. But he always maintained that the first Pernod of the evening tasted better on the boulevards than anywhere else. I never saw Morrice in evening clothes, and I doubt whether, though well enough off, he possessed a tail-coat or a dinner-jacket even. I suppose he would have been called a Bohemian. He did not look like one, he dressed *en bourgeois*: no Lavallière and wide-awake for him, but a stiff white collar of the up and down variety and a neat speckled tie. Only his head betrayed the artist, a pear-shaped, bald head with a pointed beard and slightly mad eyes. I remember saying timidly to O'Conor—timidly, for you must remember that I had only just come to Paris from Cambridge and that O'Conor was the most formidable figure in the quarter—I remember saying that I thought Morrice the most remarkable of our companions at the *Chat Blanc*. 'He's the only one who has character, if that's what you mean', growled

O'Conor. Kelly tells a story which may be true and is certainly illuminating. Early one summer morning a party was returning from a carouse when Morrice somehow or other fell into the gutter. There was nothing extraordinary in that: from time to time Morrice was knocked over by a horse and never seemed much the worse for it. But on this June morning it so happened that the gutter was a rippling stream; for they were washing the streets. There lay Morrice on his back gazing up out of the cold water into the dawn-lit sky and murmuring, with unmistakable gusto, 'pearly', 'pearly'.

O'Conor—Roderick O'Conor—was of course an Irishman. He came of a land-owning family which by his own account had done well enough out of the Land Purchase Act.[1] He was a swarthy man, with a black moustache, greying when I met him, tallish and sturdy. He carried a stick, and there was nothing Bohemian about his appearance. In 1904 he was over forty I suppose, and had not been in the British Isles for twenty years or more, so he told me. He told me too that somewhere in London he had a top-hat. He was highly intelligent and well educated, had read widely in French and English and was conversant with the Latin masters. At one time he seems to have known, if only a little, most of the more interesting French painters of his generation—the Nabi for instance: but the acquaintance had been allowed to drop. Why? I haven't a

[1]Mr. Buchanan says that O'Conor 'suffered from poverty'. This, I think, is an exaggeration. So far as I can remember O'Conor was sometimes hard up, but never poor.

notion. Sheer laziness perhaps. Misanthropic he certainly was; and I should say he was a solitary by temperament had he not taken undisguised pleasure in lunching almost daily in that autumn of 1904 with a callow youth from Cambridge, well educated to be sure and let us hope fairly intelligent. Yes, we lunched almost daily at *Le Petit Lavenne*; and, as Kelly had disappeared into Montmartre, O'Conor became my most intimate friend. He exhibited at the *Salon d'automne* and *Les Indépendants*, through which societies he must have preserved relations of some sort with the French artists. Indeed later, much later, when I was making friends with the painters of his generation and the next, I was surprised to find how often, when I pronounced his name, one of them would exclaim—'Le père O'Conor: tiens, qu'est-ce qu'il fait à présent?' What was he doing? I hardly knew how to reply, though we continued for twenty years and more to meet occasionally by appointment and dine at the *Alençon* (always in the quarter you perceive). I have suggested that he was solitary by choice; yet I remember once when I met him he said he had just returned from Italy, and added that he had stayed there picture-gazing until he began to feel lonely: evidently there was a degree of solitude which he could not stand. I suspect he was a tragic figure though he kept his tragedy to himself. Conscious of gifts—perhaps great gifts—he was conscious too that he lacked power of expression. His pictures—there is one in the room next to the study in which I am writing—were full of austere intention unrealised; incidentally, they were influenced by Cézanne at a time when the influence

of Cézanne was not widespread, when, in my part of
Montparnasse, his name was unknown. These pictures painted at the beginning of the century are
sometimes oddly like what daring young men were
to paint ten years later. His taste and judgment were
remarkable: already in 1904 he had noticed most of
those talents, plastic and literary, which in 1914 it
was still considered 'advanced' to recognise. From
time to time he would give me a book, and the authors he chose in 1904 or '5 were, if I remember
right, Claudel, Laforgue, Remy de Gourmont, Jules
Rennard and—unless I am confusing dates—Charles-
Louis Philippe. He certainly gave me, then or a little
later, the autobiography of Madame Sacher Masoch.
He was an accomplished book-hunter, and found
for me on the *quais* the 1882 large-paper edition of
Flaubert and a first edition of Mérimée's *Lettres à
une Inconnue*. His taste in pictures, if not precisely
catholic, was not as narrow as that of most painters.
He admired both Ingres and Delacroix, and must
have been one of the first to see something in the
douanier Rousseau. He spotted the *Chasse au tigre*
when it was shown at Les Indépendants and advised
me to buy it for a hundred francs. I was tempted,
but the picture seemed rather large to bring home
in a portmanteau. That he did not buy it himself
was possibly because he was hard up, probably because he had no place for it: already he possessed
paintings by Gauguin, Bonnard, Rouault and
Laprade amongst others. Of course there were
plenty of people in Paris in 1904 who knew all about
these painters and writers; but at the *Chat Blanc* I
do not think I ever heard the name of Cézanne or

Gauguin or Van Gogh pronounced. For O'Conor, when he dined there, never talked 'art', unless to deflate some overblown reputation—e.g. that of Whistler, Sargent, Conder Carrière or Cottet, all of whom passed for masters in the Anglo-American quarter. Generally he confined himself to comments on people and things, gruff and disobliging as a rule, and to grim jokes. It was only at our tête-à-tête *déjeuners*, sometimes followed by a round of the galleries, that he permitted himself a little enthusiasm about pictures and books.

The great event in O'Conor's life had been, I surmise, his friendship—a close friendship so far as I could make out—with Gauguin. They met at Pont Aven, during Gauguin's last sojourn in Brittany perhaps, or perhaps earlier; O'Conor dealt little in dates and let fall his recollections in stray sentences amidst conversations on alien topics. But I assume the friendship was pretty close because O'Conor possessed drawings by the master bearing affectionate and humorous inscriptions: also, at some time or other he lent Gauguin his studio in the rue Cherchemidi. What to me seems clear is that Gauguin's strength of character and convincing style of talk made a deep impression on the young, or youngish, Irishman, and I dare say it was the only deep impression he ever received from a fellow creature. That Gauguin had a way of talking and moving and looking which caught his imagination I feel sure: years later, in 1919 or 1920, when I invited him to meet Derain, O'Conor told me, solemnly almost, that he had never met anyone whose manner reminded him so much of Gauguin's. Now O'Conor did not much admire Derain's painting; he would have been at no pains to pay him a compliment, and assuredly he considered this judgment of his complimentary in the highest degree. So, if in his judgment Derain and Gauguin were in some subtle but significant way alike, I am inclined to believe that they were.

Pictures, books, music, drawings, photographs (mostly so far as I remember of works by Greco and Cézanne) filled O'Conor's life and his spacious but gloomy studio. He never put pen to paper if he could help it, and when obliged to do so wrote in a childish, irregular hand, rather surprising in a man of his culture and force.[1] An *amie* he had, kept severely in the background: I never saw her. The charming and gifted lady, whom I knew too little, and who mitigated the painful loneliness of his old age, can at this time have been no more than a child. He played the violin—to himself. Rarely did he make the immense effort of going to a concert, though he loved music.[2] You must remember there was no wireless in those days, and I doubt whether much classical music had been recorded for the gramophone. So he played to himself, badly. He might have bought a pianola: he did not, nor could he have dreamed of such a thing. In music his taste was austere, and he would snarl at Morrice for his 'romanticism' and 'laxity'. After a scolding from O'Conor, Morrice would say to me 'let us go tomorrow and hear some

[1]However I have ten or a dozen letters from him, some of them long and mostly about painting.

[2]Occasionally he passed an evening with Thompson listening to the piano.

lenient music', and off he would take me to hear
Traviata at the Opéra Comique. But O'Conor remained in his quarter grim and uncompromising.
Once only did I see him impressed by a human
being, and that was by Virginia Woolf—Virginia
Stephen to be exact. In 1904 she was very young
and quite unknown, having published nothing: but
O'Conor confessed after their first and, I think, only
meeting—'she put the fear of God into me'.

As I came to know more people in Paris inevitably
I saw less of Morrice and O'Conor, nevertheless I
kept well up with them till 1914. Morrice I saw for
the last time in the late autumn of that year. He
had come to London, perhaps a little panic-stricken,
but he did not stay long; for he found, so he told
me, that the only thing to be done in an English
winter was to sit indoors drinking whisky: 'it was
always like that' he added. So he returned to France
and improved his acquaintance with Matisse. Again
they were together in North Africa. Matisse appreciated Morrice's painting and felt his charm, but I
think he may have been disconcerted by his habits.
He did not like it, I gather, when the Arab urchins
took to following Morrice in the street shouting
'Whisky, Whisky'. When I returned to Paris in 1919
I tried to find Morrice. No one seemed to know
where he was; only it was thought that he was rarely
in town. Occasionally I heard tell of him from
O'Conor; stories were repeated by Matisse or by
Georges Duthuit; but it was not until I read Mr.
Buchanan's book that I knew that he had died in
Tunis in January 1924.

One day, in the late 'twenties' I suppose, I was

to lunch with Segonzac who was serving on the hanging committee of the *salon d'automne*. I chanced to fall in with O'Conor who had sent pictures to the exhibition and suggested that he should join the party. Segonzac said it would be delightful to see 'le père O'Conor' again, and as usual the qualification surprised me: I never thought of O'Conor in that way. Segonzac insisted on lunching *chez* 'Footit', an English bar kept by an ex-clown, or rather by an ex-clown's wife, which suited the taste of the French in a certain mood. It was *bien anglais*—it was indeed: a tough, over-cooked chop, watery potatoes and a bottle of tepid beer, to be consumed at a high counter instead of a table: *bien anglais*. O'Conor and Segonzac went back to the *Petit Palais*, and I stayed in the hope of getting into conversation with two pretty English girls who were manifestly out of their depth. Was that the last time I saw O'Conor? No, now I come to think of it, I saw him some years later, one Sunday afternoon when I was drinking a solitary *café crême* at *les deux Magots*: O'Conor and his amie passed by and stopped to have a word with me. That was the last. He went to live in the midi, married his mistress, and—so Matthew Smith tells me—died a good while ago.

X

PARIS IN 'THE TWENTIES'

STRANGE as it seems today, and will seem to future generations, in 1919 there were intelligent men and women who believed that an age of peace and prosperity lay before mankind. I hasten to say that I was not one of them. Like most people, however, I was happy, and there was much to be happy about. The war was over, that was the great thing. The slaughter, the hardship, the dictatorship of the press—for that is what government amounted to in the last years—the reign of terror and stupidity was over—for the time being. Once again civilized people in England would be allowed to lead civilized lives; and obviously one of the things they would wish to regain would be contact with civilized people in other countries. They would want to travel. As it happened, continental civilization came to us before we had a chance of going to it; for early in the summer of 1919 Diaghileff's troupe arrived in London, with *La Boutique fantasque* and *Le Tricorne*, with Picasso, Derain, Stravinsky and Ansermet, imparting, as the Russian ballet always did, its own culture and collecting its own public, both of which were international. Suddenly the arts became the preoccupation of Society (with the capital S) which twelve months earlier had been preoccupied with military and political intrigues. French became the language of the Savoy where Diaghileff, Massine,

Stravinsky, Picasso and Picasso's very beautiful and rather aristocratic wife were staying for the season. Abruptly and unexpectedly the wheels of civilization began to turn.

Picasso dwelt in the Savoy: for Derain we found a modest lodging in Regent's Square; and their ways of life in London were as distinct as their addresses. Madame Picasso had no notion of joining in the rough and tumble of even upper Bohemia. She and her husband lived in their fashionable hotel and went to fashionable parties, at which, if they happened to be evening parties, the latter appeared 'en smoking'. Derain never went beyond a blue serge suit. Even on the first night of *La Boutique*—and never before or since have I beheld such a scene of white-tied, tail-coated enthusiasm—when at last Diaghileff and Massine forced him in front of the curtain Derain was still wearing that suit; so inevitably he was wearing it at the extremely smart supper-party given afterwards in his honour. I remember coming home from that party, Derain, Ansermet and I in a 'taxi', all the better for the evening may be, and driving round and round Gordon Square pursuing some momentous argument about I know not what. Ansermet, I should explain, who had come to conduct the orchestra, played a leading part in the adventures and festivities of that memorable summer.

The Picassos, I have said, went mostly to fashionable parties; however they went to one that was pretty shabby. I shared a house then—number 46 Gordon Square—with Maynard Keynes, who early in the year had gone to Paris for the peace-conference, out of which he had walked in a state of well justified indignation. He and I decided that for once Picasso should meet a few of the unfashionable. We, in our turn, would give a supper-party. From the ballet we invited the Picassos, Derain, Lopokova and Ansermet. We did not invite Diaghileff; but we did invite some forty young or youngish painters, writers and students—male and female. Maynard, Duncan Grant, our two maids and I waited on them. Picasso did not dress. We rigged up a couple of long tables: at the end of one we put Ansermet, at the end of the other Lytton Strachey, so that their beards might wag in unison. I remember that Aldous Huxley brought with him a youth called Drieu La Rochelle—that ill-starred and gifted writer, whose memory it seems is still under a cloud, but whom I, for my part, shall never cease to regret.

This London prelude to Paris in 'the twenties' was necessary because, when I went to Paris for a couple of months or more in the autumn of 1919, intending to see pictures and old friends, I made a host of new ones; and with most of these new friends—my friends of 'the twenties'—I became acquainted through Derain whom I met for the first time that summer in London. With Picasso my acquaintance was older, though it was never so intimate. I had known him since 1911 or thereabouts. I believe it was Gertrude Stein who took me to his studio overlooking the *cimetière Montparnasse*: I remember Picasso said he liked the view. (This, by the way, should help to fix a date—I never knew Picasso in Montmartre). Gertrude Stein and her brother Leo were then living together in the rue Fleurus and collecting pictures by Matisse and Picasso. It was mere chance —so at least it has always seemed to me—that they were not collecting works by Monsieur Untel and his gifted sister: for neither, so far as I could make out, had a genuine feeling for visual art. Miss Stein, as everyone knows, became a famous patron—a valuable patron at a critical moment she certainly was —and a famous propounder of riddles. Leo took to psycho-analysis and Futurism and had his day of notoriety. The truth seems to be that they were a pair of theorists—Leo possessing the better brain and Gertrude the stronger character, and that for them pictures were pegs on which to hang hypotheses. They took up Matisse and Picasso; but, as I have dared to suggest, they might just as well have taken up something quite different, something that provided an even better peg. And, in fact, Leo did take up the Italian Futurists, while Gertrude took up Sir Francis Rose. It was their brother, or cousin perhaps, Michael who loved painting; and it was in his house, in the rue Madame, before the first war, that I saw a superb collection of early Matisse—up to 1912 say —which enabled me to follow and appreciate the development of that master's art.

Having mentioned Matisse, may I elongate a digression which is perhaps pardonable in a chapter even more discursive than those which have gone before, and speak of our first meeting and tell a tale. For Matisse, too, I met before the 1914–18 war; whereas in 'the twenties' I saw very little of him. I was taken to his studio at Clamart by Bréal and Simon Bussy: Roger Fry was of the party. I remember the pictures, and I remember a small conservatory full of exquisite flowers which often provided 'motifs' for those pictures; but of the artist himself, as he appeared at that first meeting, I remember very little. Much later I came to know him fairly well, and I shall try to give some account of him in the course of this memoir. But already, at the time of which for the moment I am writing (about 1912 or '13) he must have been famous and prosperous too, for he had taken to riding in the Bois —in brown top-boots. And thereby hangs the tale. It is one that Matisse used himself to tell, so there can be no harm in repeating it. Those who have seen him will realise that Matisse had not the figure for equitation; and one day what you would have expected to happen did happen: he fell off. He was a little—a very little—hurt; he took a cab and drove straight to the family doctor; then he drove home. Meanwhile the doctor had telephoned to Madame Matisse—but this of course Matisse did not know—to say that the injury amounted to nothing. 'Reassure him', said the doctor, 'his is a sensitive, nervous disposition; reassure him'. At this moment Matisse in his cab was making up his mind to be brave. He would belittle the accident. He felt rather grand about this, about the attitude he intended to adopt—he told the story himself you must remember—and so feeling reached his own door to be greeted by wife and daughter with cries of 'C'est rien, Henri', 'C'est rien, papa', 'le docteur dit que c'est rien'. It was a disappointing reception, you must admit, to one who had steeled himself for the rôle of stiff-lipped hero.

To return to my theme—Paris in 'the twenties',

which for my purpose begin in November 1919: it was then that *Les deux Magots* was in its glory. Derain was the presiding genius and Alice Derain the lovely and gracious queen. Braque and Madame Braque were faithful clients; André Salmon and Madame Salmon seldom failed to appear; Bernouard, the little printer who produced those elegant editions under the sign of *La rose de France*, never. Bernouard seemed to have known everyone and to have been present on all memorable occasions. Once I asked Cocteau how this could be, seeing that Bernouard was still young and had never been very important. He was so small, said Cocteau, that he slipped between everyone's legs and secured a front seat. Oberlé, the poet Gabory, the painter Gerbaud, came often to the apéritif; Segonzac and Despiau sometimes; Jean Marchand, Kisling, Marcoussis rarely; and when they chanced to be in Paris, Stravinsky and Ansermet dropped in. But these two I see most clearly at a restaurant in the rue Bonaparte where we sometimes dined. I recall with surprising distinctness—had I the gift I could make a drawing of the scene—a side room on a hot Sunday afternoon in the early 'twenties'. There we had lunched, and there we were sitting on and on, drinking tepid, sweet champagne, and moving round and round the table to dodge the sun that somehow would keep poking in. We—'we' were Derain and Alice, Stravinsky, Ansermet, an English lady and myself—we stayed because Derain had fallen into argument with Stravinsky about music. Ansermet joined the fray. And so great that afternoon was Stravinsky's lucidity and power of expression, or maybe so heady

the wine, that for once in my life, and once only, I
fancied that I understood music. Other musicians I
remember meeting at the *Magots* were Satie and
(once or twice) Poulenc. But it was not in my quarter that 'les six' were to be found: them I came to
know (one intimately, the others slightly) through
Jean Cocteau, and I associate them with *Le Boeuf
sur le toit* and Cocteau's Saturday dinners.

In this exciting and delightful autumn—delightful it was though I believe it rained, and sometimes
snowed as well, every day almost, I renewed my
friendship with Copeau and Vildrac, whom Roger
Fry had enticed to London in 1911 to represent 'the
modern movement' in French literature and drama
at the Post-Impressionist exhibition; and through
them I met one or two writers and actors—Gide,
Duhamel, Luc Durtain, Jules Romains, Jouvet: the
enchanting Valentine Tessier I had already come
to know and admire in London. None of these was
ever to be seen at *Les Magots*. On the other hand,
Léger, Lipchitz and Madame Lipchitz, Pascin and
Metzinger made, I am inclined to think, rare appearances; certainly in the 'twenties' I knew them
all, slightly. They were not, however, of the set to
which I had been admitted—*la bande à Derain* as I
believe it was called sometimes; neither were the
dealers Zborowski and Basler who were often to be
seen on the terrace and whom of course we knew.
Basler was a figure of fun, a small Polish Jew with
a bowler hat, who had taken on himself the sacred
duty of making known the genius of a compatriot
called Coubine. The story went that a delegation
which had come to buy modern pictures for War-

saw visited Basler's gallery, his attic to be exact, and having made some purchases, refused to buy a work by the protégé. In vain Basler implored. 'We have exhausted our credit' explained the tactful leader of the mission. 'Then', exclaimed Basler, trusting into unwilling arms a substantial canvas by the neglected master, 'then accept this as a tribute from La France.' Zborowski, another Pole, was a different sort of dealer. Cultivated and comely, he wrote poetry in his spare time, and was the friend of painters and poets. He dealt especially in Modigliani and Soutine, both of whom he knew well and helped generously—neither of whom (alas!) did I ever meet. He was also on the best of terms with Max Jacob, whom I did know fairly well.

It was some time in November that I first met, through the English dealer P. M. Turner, an artist who, I am happy to say, remains one of my great friends. Dunoyer de Segonzac is, as everyone knows, a painter of class—in my opinion his water-colours, pen-drawings and etchings are even better than his oils: he is also one of the most charming men alive. He is my notion of a gentleman of Gascony, and he has a way with him that gets away with anything. Stories in proof of this abound: for instance, it is told how, on his first visit to England, staying at a hotel in Mayfair, he came down to breakfast and demanded what he understood from the writings of Sir Walter Scott to be the correct fare—beef and beer. The head-waiter tried to explain that the serving of such a meal at such an hour in the coffee-room was not only unusual but inadmissible. All would not do: Segonzac had his way, that is to say his flagon of ale and cut off the cold sirloin. And only the other day—I record the incident to show that Segonzac has not lost the art of wheedling—returning with me after lunch to my hotel in the rue Condé he exclaimed—'Why, next door is my grandmother's house, where I played on Sunday afternoons as a child; I must show you over it'. Sure enough, he rang the bell, cajoled the old woman who answered it, and to the surprise, but also pleasure, of the tenants made a tour of their rooms describing exactly what was done in them and how it was done sixty years ago. In the 'twenties' Segonzac came sometimes to the *Magots* for an apéritif and every now and then stayed to dine with us. For you must not suppose that these gatherings ended at eight o'clock. As many as nine or ten—*la bande à Derain*—would go on to some bistrot or modest restaurant (Michaud, Establet or a place near *les halles de vins*) where, all other customers having retired, sometimes we ended the evening in song.

Othon Friesz, in whose house in la rue Notre Dame des Champs I have spent many pleasant evenings, never came to the *Magots*. I believe he had his own good reasons for not joining our party. So I believe had Vlaminck. He, as everybody knows, had a magnificent painting-gift, which, as some of us think, he squandered; and Friesz, too, never quite fulfilled his promise—at one moment he was amongst the most admired of the fauves. Vlaminck has written a couple of books which reveal a literary talent not to be denied; it is less generally known that Friesz too, could write effectively and wittily when he gave his mind to it: I doubt, however, whether he published anything more substantial than an article or preface.

Twice, and twice only, in my life did I meet James Joyce, and our first encounter was on the terrace of this famous café—still famous, or as some think infamous, haunted by Existentionalists and crowded with tourists who come to see Existentionalists drink. This meeting was not memorable; the second, if the sitting of two people at the same table without exchanging a word can be called a meeting, was at least on a memorable occasion. Kind Mr. Shiff gave a supper-party in honour of Diaghileff after the first night in Paris of some ballet or other. He invited forty or fifty guests, members of the ballet and friends of the ballet, painters, writers, dress-makers and ladies of fashion; but that on which he had set his heart was to assemble at his hospitable board— in an upper room at the Majestic—the four living men he most admired: Picasso, Stravinsky, Joyce and Proust. About netting the first two there was no difficulty: they pertained to the ballet. But when we sat down to supper, well after midnight, there was no sign of Joyce or Proust. However, about coffee-time, appeared in the midst of the elegantly dressed throng someone dressed otherwise, someone a good deal the worse for wear. It turned out to be Joyce. He seemed far from well. Certainly he was in no mood for supper. But a chair was set for him on our host's right, and there he remained speechless with his head in his hands and a glass of champagne in front of him. Between two and three o'clock appeared, to most people's surprise I imagine, a small dapper figure, not 'dressed' to be sure, but clad in exquisite black with white kid gloves. It was Proust of course. He entered in the manner of one who should say 'I was passing by and happened to see a light in your room, so I just dropped in to shake hands'. He was given a chair on his host's left, and found himself next Stravinsky to whom, in his polite way, he tried to make himself agreeable. 'Doubtless you admire Beethoven', he began. 'I detest Beethoven' was all he got for answer. 'But, cher maître, surely those late sonatas and quartets . . . ?' 'Pires que les autres' growled Stravinsky. Ansermet intervened in an attempt to keep the peace; there was no row but the situation was tense. Joyce began to snore—I hope it was a snore. Marcelle Meyer, who sat next me, suggested that the Avenue de Breteuil lay not so far out of my way, which was hardly true, but I jumped at the excuse. Of course I should be delighted to drop her home; Mr. Shiff would understand; besides it really was very late.

How that party ended I have never cared to enquire; but it reminds me of another encounter with fame, in some ways similar. One Sunday in the late 'twenties' Nils de Dardel invited me to lunch in his studio on the heights of Montmartre—in la rue Lepic I fancy. It was a small party: Nils and his charming wife, Marcel Herrand, one or two more I suppose. Isadora Duncan was expected; but when she arrived, at the end of lunch, all she felt up to was a large glass of brandy. Having disposed of that, she fell back on the sofa and drew down beside her the first male object she could lay hands on, which happened to be me. Then, taking one of my hands, she ran it lovingly over her person, murmuring the while, by way of excuse and in a strong American accent—'Je ne suis pas une femme, je suis un génie'. So she continued for some time, long enough at any rate for Nils to whip out his water-colours and sketch the scene. That drawing used to hang in my flat at 50 Gordon Square, and if I can find it I will publish it, 'to witness if I lie'.[1]

The one person never to be seen at Les deux Magots, nor at any other gathering of painters unless it were a private view or a first night, was Picasso. He lived apart, with his lady-wife and his little son Polo, in the rue la Boëtie above Paul Rosenberg's shop. There I used to visit him of a morning. As you may suppose, I was shy of disturbing the great artist at that time of day; but he would say 'drop in any time in the morning—besides no one ever caught me working'. And true it is I have rarely seen Picasso at work. I saw him make a drawing of which I shall have a word to say; in London, I saw him add a few touches to his curtain for *Le Tricorne*; and once I saw him do something to a plate in his pottery at Valauris. But I have seen him watching others work. One day when I called workmen were painting and graining a big *porte cochère* on the opposite side of the street. Picasso was fascinated. The elaboration of the technique enchanted him. He explained to me what they were about and that they were only at the beginning of their job (I had imagined that it was nearly finished). No, they would go on adding coats of paint and letting them dry; and then would come the delicate business of

[1]I have found it.

regraining and varnishing. It would take days. And so far as I could make out Picasso intended to stay at the window till it was done.

As I have said, in the years after his first marriage Picasso lived apart and saw more of the fashionable world than of pre-war acquaintances. But I recall a luncheon-party in his flat—a rare event—in the autumn of 1920 perhaps, to which were invited Derain, Jean Cocteau, Satie and myself. After lunch we were set in a row, for all the world as though we were posing for the village photographer, and Picasso 'took our likenesses'. I wish I could get hold of that drawing or a reproduction even. Years ago I asked Picasso what had become of it. He felt sure it was not lost; but as to where it was, of that he was far from sure: probably somewhere in the studio, not easily to be come at. Now, however, that he has two or three secretaries at his beck and call surely it should be possible to hunt it down.

Picasso kept himself to himself in the 'twenties'. I saw him from time to time in his studio or in the fashionable or quasi-fashionable world, at parties which generally had something to do with the ballet; for of the Russian ballet Olga Picasso was a loyal supporter. I remember pleasant lunches with him and Cocteau, Madame Picasso being sometimes of the party. She liked discreet places such as La Pérouse or Voisin, but was not averse from an occasional evening at 'Le Boeuf sur le toit', which, if not discreet, was gay and tolerably smart. And, having named this restaurant, may I, before describing it, take the opportunity of contradicting a lie which the name puts me in mind of? It is a paltry lie but vexatious. I should have scotched it long ago, but, being lazy, I procrastinated; and as it still rankles I will get the humour off my chest at the risk of being thought touchy and of wandering from my subject. The late Lord Derwent, under the pseudonym 'George Vandan' or 'Vanden'—Vandan or Vanden was I believe one of his Christian names—some years since published a book the name of which I forget; and in that book gave his version of a party at *Le Boeuf*. His version is incorrect. Here are the facts. Peter Johnstone, as he then was, longed to meet Picasso, and pestered me to bring about a meeting. I will commit almost any folly to avoid being pestered, or, when unescapably cornered, to bring the affliction to an end. I invited him to meet Picasso and Madame Picasso at dinner. I was not drunk: I see no harm in being tipsy on suitable occasions, but on this occasion it happens I was not. I did not pay Picasso extravagant compliments: our relations were not of a kind in which compliments are paid face to face. In any case I do not think Lord Derwent could have known what was Picasso's impression of the evening, for, to the best of my knowledge, they did not meet again for years—if ever. I suppose Picasso felt no call to improve the acquaintance.

Madame, I have said, preferred discreet restaurants; but I must not forget an evening on which a lady of whom both were fond enticed them with my help to dinner in Montmartre—on the Place du Tertre if you please. Recalling the event—for an event it was—I realise that as early as 'the twenties' Picasso had become a legendary figure. I shall not forget the date either, for not only was it Sunday,

Sunday in June, but Whit-Sunday, *La Pentecôte*. The streets were full of saunterers; the *Place* was packed; tables crept out into the road. It was beginning to look as though our plot to lure the shy master into the open would be foiled by a coincidence, when I had the luck to espy a free table by the door of a bistrot. Slowly, very slowly, we were served by a little boy with a genuine Montmartrois accent; and the accent maybe reminded Picasso of old days in the rue Ravignan. At any rate he seemed to take pleasure in making the child prattle. His spirits rose, he became wittier than ever, and I began to count on a late sitting. But it was Picasso—Picasso the legendary. It may have been as much as ten years since he was last seen outside or inside a bistrot. People eyed our table. There was whispering: 'c'est Picasso'. One or two almost forgotten acquaintances —whom I did not know—came up and shook hands. Madame became restless. It was time to call for the bill. So we too began to saunter. We sauntered down the hill towards the rue La Boëtie, and, as we were passing the Gare St. Lazare, Picasso, turning to his hostess, said 'Would you like to be shown over the station? It is one of the finest sights in Paris'. Stupidly I demurred: it was late, I said, and the better part of the station would be closed or in darkness at all events. So I shall never know what beauties and curiosities Picasso had discovered in the Gare St. Lazrae; and serve me right.

Now I must try to describe *Le Boeuf sur le toit*. This restaurant, café, café-chantant and 'dancing' combined was invented by Jean Cocteau and began life, modestly enough, as, unless I mistake, *La Cigogne*, in the rue Duphot. Soon, having become well known and much frequented, it migrated to roomier quarters in the rue Boissy d'Anglas. Here Cocteau reigned supreme. He made of it a sort of G.H.Q. for *Les six*—the six musicians: Darius Milhaud, Poulenc, Auric, Honneger, Germaine Taillefer and Marcelle Meyer. I believe I have named them correctly, though it seems odd that neither Satie nor Sauguet should have been of the company. The *Boeuf* cannot be described properly as a night-club or a 'dancing' though people did dance and drink champagne there, sometimes till four o'clock in the morning. But people also lunched there quietly, and dined unobtrusively in a side room. Of an afternoon you might find writers and journalists who wished to discuss seriously an article or a scene in a play, and in a corner some young American correcting proofs. Shabby painters dropped in for a look round at any hour of the day or night. Nevertheless it was smart; it was 'the place to go to', and a peculiar section of Tout Paris, Tout Londres and Tout New York went. English visitors would come straight from the train, sure of finding there someone they knew, some friend or friends with whom to make dates. It was a fashionable meeting-place, but peaceful enough till six o'clock in the evening.

After six the *Boeuf* became immensely gay and light-hearted. It was a 'show' in itself—a show in which waiters and chasseurs played their parts, while the girl who sold nosegays by the cloakroom door was always pretty and never stayed long. At the piano would be some hard up youth of talent, destined for fame—Wiener at one time. Freyel might

sing. Rubinstein might suddenly take it into his head
to play. On the floor were some of the most elegant
women and best dancers in Paris. The décor, always
amusing, was subject to surprising changes. For instance, struck by the decorative effect of fly-posters
stuck all over the town advertising a concert and
bearing on pink paper the single word 'RUBIN-
STEIN', Cocteau had printed fly-posters bearing
the names of favoured clients and stuck them all
over the café and restaurant. In discreet but magis-
terial control of all was the inimitable Moyse.

Gradually the *Boeuf* became one of those places,
which perhaps still exist in Paris, where the beau
monde and the ragamuffins can drop clan-conscious-
ness and mingle happily—more or less. And so it
remained for half a dozen years or more. In the
middle 'twenties' at any rate it was both fashionable
and what, for want of a better English word, I must
call Bohemian. Sometimes 'en smoking' with my
more elegant friends, French, English and American, sometimes in tweeds—en ragamuffin in fact—
with the painters, I have spent merry nights in the
rue Boissy d'Anglas. To be sure the painters affected
to despise the place, declaring that it was too *chic*,
and too dear and stank of American cigarettes
which, however, they always smoked when given
the chance. Nevertheless I have had as much fun
there with Derain, Segonzac, Villeboeuf and Kisling, as with Arthur Rubinstein and his decorative
public. And it was there that I heard Picasso (still
in the dinner-jacket period) deliver one of those
utterances as characteristically Picassonian as the
sentences of the majestic doctor are characteristic-

ally Johnsonian. Cocteau was at the time composing that briiliant piece, *Orphée*, and, turning to Picasso with whom I was sitting, enquired—'Do you see any objection to a miracle on the stage? I want to bring a miracle into my play'. 'A miracle', said Picasso, 'there's nothing surprising about a miracle. Why it's a miracle every morning that I don't melt in my bath'. Dare I add Derain's comment on this flight of fancy when I repeated it to him? 'A few years ago it would have been a greater miracle if Picasso had taken a bath at any hour of the day'.

Of all the French painters who illustrated the 'twenties' Derain was the one I knew best: he was the only one whom I 'tutoyed'. Of his art I have written elsewhere at length. It was as various as that of any artist of his time, and, like the little girl with the curl in the middle of her forehead, 'when it was good it was very, very good'. In the 'thirties' and 'forties' he painted plenty of bad pictures, and in consequence his art was decried. Now justice is being done by the more thoughtful critics, for instance by Mr. Douglas Cooper and Mr. Denys Sutton. I wonder what has become of the decorations he made for Halvorsen's dining-room: ballet décors apart, they are, I suspect, his finest achievement. But perhaps it was his character that most impressed his friends; it seemed exactly suited to his height and tremendous frame and noble Roman head. He was a man of natural authority, which he exerted without a glimmer of self-consciousness. He spoke slowly, as beseemed his bulk, and with distinction and humour; though a habit of talking with a pipe in his mouth sometimes muffled his voice and distressed his friends. Two stories may give a better notion of his character and style than any analysis of which I am capable.

I was walking with Derain in Seven Dials, where, at the time of *La Boutique fantasque*, he had a studio, or rather a floor above a warehouse—I think it was a warehouse. A stranger approached me and asked the way to some hotel with the name of which I was unfamiliar. Derain promptly took the matter in hand. With a magnificent gesture and sounds which presumably he took to be English words he indicated a direction. The authority was superb and it inspired absolute confidence. The stranger marched off, completely satisfied it seemed, down a street towards which the impressive arm was pointing. When he was gone Derain informed me with undiminished authority that the hotel he was seeking was 'The Shaftesbury': it did not sound in the least like that nor did what Derain said to me sound much like 'Shaftesbury'. However that was what he had in mind. He knew the place well, he said. Whether the stranger ever reached it we shall never know.

And here is another story that may help those who knew him not to savour Derain's character. It was decided at *Les Deux Magots* that Rubinstein should meet Kisling, since these two—who had never met—were reckoned amongst the greater glories of their country. They were to meet at the café after dinner. Now Arthur Rubinstein, who, besides being a great pianist, is a delightful companion, has or had this drawback: he took his public about with him. That was not his fault: his admirers adhered to him. Often their presence added to the pleasure of his company; for amongst his faithful followers were many attractive women and men both sensitive and intelligent. But there were others. On this Sunday evening arrived with Rubinstein in fullest evening dress two tall 'rastas' from South America with what Derain called their 'poules de luxe'. The meeting at the *Magots* was not a success; so unsuccessful was it that very soon Rubinstein invited those who would to come with him for a drink chez Fox. Fox was 'a character', of English descent presumably, who kept a small café-restaurant (a snack-bar they would call it now) near the Gare St-Lazare. A dozen of us perhaps, including the four South Americans, took cabs and crossed the river. Chez Fox the two rastas behaved abominably. They insulted the old *patron* and his waiter, called them spies, pulled out Fox's tie, and finally pelted his looking glass and bottles with the hard-boiled eggs that lay in a basket on the counter. They were not drunk: they were simply hubristic; they were rich and they were bloody. (I am bound to say they paid for the damage). I could see that Derain was furious. Rubinstein I make no doubt suffered acutely. But Derain took action, that is to say he took my hand, observing—'as you know, I have the gift of reading a man's future in his hand: I will tell your fortune'. He proceeded to foretell the most exciting and improbable adventures for me and for two or three more of his friends, accompanied by caustic comments on our characters and habits. The South Americans stopped throwing eggs and crowded round him. Of course they all wished to have their fortunes told. Derain took the hand of the taller and handsomer of the two men and gazed on it with terrifying intensity. Then in calm but awe-inspiring tones pronounced—'No: I dare not tell you what I see there'. The effect was magical; I could hardly believe my eyes. He had frightened the rastas out of their wits. They fled; and I suppose Rubinstein felt bound to accompany his public. But Derain, turning to Fox, said 'Now we will all have supper, and you and your waiter shall be our guests. I dare say there's plenty to eat in the house: I can see a few eggs still intact: anyhow there's plenty of wine. The evening ended as well as it had begun badly.

If I were to name all the odd and eminent Parisians I met in 'the twenties' but never came to know well, this chapter would grow as tedious as the social column of *The Times*—some may think it would not have far to go. For instance, one summer I did come to know Dufy quite well; for we used to lunch together of a Sunday in a restaurant near his studio in the Impasse Guelma. To my shame I have no vivid recollections of his conversation. I remember that he was an agreeable companion, and that his atelier was of an extraordinary neatness and factory-like precision. There was a room for silks and a room for cottons and a room for painting pictures, and in all his operations were so neat and cleanly that one felt he could have executed them in a drawing-room. Of the charm of his work, especially of his textiles, I need not speak: everyone knows them, and most people of taste admire. Another artist whom I wish I had known better was Christian Bérard. I used to meet him with Cocteau and later at our Embassy: once or twice he dined with me.

He was both eminent and odd, and in my opinion, one of the best stage-decorators of our time. And then there was that great man Rouault. Only once did I meet him; I sat next to him at dinner, but all he said, and kept on saying, was 'on ne peut pas dire que Vollard me tient', from which I concluded that Vollard le tenait. He is a great artist, but he might have been a greater. Apparently, some time early in the century, he gave up looking at things and invented clichés. There was a formula for Dives and a formula for Lazarus: clowns, judges, tycoons, saints, sinners and divine persons, he had them all taped. Trusting to his imagination and skill he has played beautifully with his formulae these forty years; but I wish he would sometimes go out of doors and look about him.

One of the people I met in Paris in 'the twenties' has become a life-long friend—Georges Duthuit. But to describe all the fun we have had, together and in company, in Paris and in London, in Barcelona, Venice and Aix-en-Provence, would need fifty pages and a pen more picturesque than mine. When he comes to write my obituary notice in *Nice-Matin*—I count on him for that—I hope he will not forget the racing fleas of Montparnasse nor Aldous Huxley's wry smile at Barcelona.

If, in the 'twenties' and 'thirties' I saw a good deal of Picasso, since the war I have seen little. That is explicable. Picasso, as all the world knows, is become a 'monument historique'. To reach him one must slip past secretaries on sentry-duty and the last time I penetrated the defences of his studio I should not have been surprised if someone had invited me to fill up a card stating the object of my visit and the number of my passport. But I do see him from time to time, and since the war I have spent a long afternoon with him which I like to remember because I found him unchanged, that is to say, witty, charming, affectionate, and quite unlike anyone else. It happened in this way. I was dining with the Simon Bussys in their flat at Nice. The party, if I remember right, besides our host and hostess and daughter (Janie Bussy), were Mrs. St. John Hutchinson, Roger Martin du Gard and myself. It was a Friday evening. Someone said—'What fun to surprise Picasso in his pottery at Vallauris'. A surprise visit it had to be for no one could discover the telephone number. So next morning off we went by omnibus, Mrs. Hutchinson, Simon Bussy and I, and after many enquiries found the pretty little pottery with its slightly medieval air, to learn that the master was not at home but was expected in the afternoon. Clearly the sensible thing to do was to lunch somewhere in the village, then sit in the sun and wait; and that is what we did. Soon to us appeared this curious cortège: first Picasso, marching, in an old grey sweater and espadrilles; next, a handsome black car, driven by a chauffeur, otherwise empty; then a troupe of workmen and girls most of whom seemed to have questions to put which the master found no difficulty in answering. I have rarely seen Picasso surprised; but when he saw us sitting in a row on the ground, or rather on my coat, his surprise was unmistakable. Also unmistakable was his pleasure at seeing Mrs. Hutchinson, an old friend, whom he had not met since before the war. The sun

blazed, Picasso was at his best, our courage and
enterprise were rewarded. None of us had seen the
pots, nor had we the faintest idea what they would
be like; for they had not yet been shown or photo-
graphed nor, I think, had anything been written
about them. As you may suppose, it was our turn
to be surprised. I thought, and think, those pots
extraordinary. Returning, we broke the journey at
Antibes, to see the paintings presented to the museum, which was closed—by now it was evening—
but opened instantly at the magic name. That, I
think, was the last time I saw Picasso as he should
be seen; but I do not despair of seeing him so again.
Matisse in the 'twenties' and 'thirties' I did not see
often. I met him now and then, and once or twice
he wrote to me about things I had written about
him: these, I suppose, had been translated by Janie
Bussy. Since the war I have been more fortunate;
I have seen him in Paris and whenever I was in the
midi I made a point of calling as I was told he liked
visits. At the time of his death I felt I had known
him well enough to correct a few of the more glaring
errors that occurred in *The Times'* obituary notice.
One visit, when he was living at Vence, is perhaps
worth recording. It was in the spring of '48. He was
in bed but he did not seem ill; indeed he said of
himself 'I am not a sick man, I am a wounded man
—"un grand mutilé".' Of a morning he still worked
a little in his studio, and in the afternoon lay in bed
cutting out those marvellous paper decorations and
drawing. (By the way, or partly by the way, I noticed a picture by Picasso on the wall). His guide,
philosopher and friend, Madame Lydia, showed us

his latest paintings, and he himself showed drawings for *Jazz* and the *Portuguese Nun*. 'Us', I say, because an English lady, to whom Matisse was deeply attached, was also paying a visit. With her, while Madame Lydia was showing me more drawings, he held a private colloquy, in which, it seems, he spoke feelingly of his life, ambitions and achievements, of his hopes and fears, in fact of 'life, death and the grand Forever'. His friend was touched, naturally, and possibly flattered. Who would not have been? Breathes there a woman with soul so dead . . . ? So it must have been a little disappointing when, some days later, at the Gare du Nord, she bought the *Figaro Littéraire* and discovered that precisely the same confidences had been imparted to a journalist who had been accorded an interview a day or two before her visit.

I saw Matisse several times in '51 and I must have seen him later: but the last visit I recall was in the spring of that year, when he was in bed at the hôtel Regina at Cimiez. I remember that Simon Bussy who was with me teased him into a perhaps unprofitable argument about religious art, during which it looked for a moment as though there had been only two religious painters. Fra Angelico was the other. On the ceiling above his bed—it was a very high room indeed—I noticed with surprise several characteristic drawings. 'How did you make them?' I enquired. 'With a fishing-rod' replied Matisse. And so he sent me off, with a note to the Mother Superior, to see his not quite finished chapel at Vence. It is finished now, and, though far from being the best thing Matisse ever did, that chapel deserves a visit. But may I advise anyone who contemplates making the pilgrimage to choose a sunny day?

INDEX

INDEX

INDEX

INDEX

INDEX

The following books are also available in
Cassell biographies.

For information about these and other books
write to the publishers at the address on
page (iv) of this book.

JOHNSON AND BOSWELL
The story of their lives

with an introduction by
Michael Holroyd

**'It would be hard to find a better introduction
to the Johnson-Boswell saga ... he has got all
the best known things in, and many of the
lesser known as well.'**
Times Literary Supplement

In writing this lively account of one of the most
famous partnerships in English literature
Hesketh Pearson presents an unusual double
biography, the story of Samuel Johnson and *his*
biographer, James Boswell.
He has drawn upon all the trustworthy
contemporary accounts. Boswell's Journals of
course, but also those of Mrs Thrale, Fanny
Burney, Anna Seward and Frances Reynolds.
Some of these are more intimate and more
revealing than Boswell, and Pearson is able to
present Dr Johnson from many points of view.
In telling Boswell's own story he presents a
skilful interpretation in spite of Boswell's
confused picture of himself.

**'Pearson is an expert at the job, readability is
his forte; he couldn't write a dull page if he
tried.'**
TLS

0 304 31440 4

THE PUPPET SHOW
OF MEMORY

'A classic autobiography'.
Dictionary of National Biography

'Memory selects with artistry and careless skill
the sights and sounds that are best worth
remembering'. So Baring begins and unfolds
for the reader a marvellous parade of
memories: childhood in a London square and
at a great country house in the 1880s; Eton and
Cambridge, followed by high spirits and
elegant company in the embassies of Paris,
Rome and Copenhagen.

In 1904, as Russia and Japan were drifting into
war, he resigned diplomacy and set out for St
Petersburg 'to study Russia thoroughly and to
make the most of my knowledge'.

There followed a nine-day train journey to
Manchuria as Reuter's correspondent and grim
adventures with the Siberian army. Baring
travelled in Russia until 1914 and won an
intimate knowledge of the social and
intellectual life in the years before the
Revolution.

It is all told with the style, subtlety and
humour that reveal a man with a genius for
friendship that keeps his memory alive today.

0 304 31444 7

SIR WALTER SCOTT

'Buchan brings to his study just that trained historical imagination which by placing Scott accurately in his time and place shows us the real man in the comprehensiveness of his genius'.
Times Literary Supplement

John Buchan's novels are so evocative of Scottish landscape and his tales so much a part of Border storytelling that he brings special insight and experience to this biography of Sir Walter Scott.
He writes with affection about the sickly youth and the disappointed lover whose writing brought him fame and prosperity in Edinburgh and London. The sad decline into illness, bankruptcy and poverty is told with sympathy but it is above all Buchan's description of Scott's novels that are the gems of this book. They reveal the genius that produced books enduring enough to give a name to a railway station, Waverley, and to a football team 'Heart of Midlothian.'

'The almost inspired literary criticisms of Sir Walter Scott show Buchan at his best.'
Dictionary of National Biography

0 304 31437 4

VICTORIA AND DISRAELI

'Mr Theo Aronson has given the best
impression of the Queen that I have read.
With much subtlety – and dead-pan humour –
he has used her relationship with Disraeli to
give us an insight into what she was really
like. His book is bright with intelligence and
human wisdom. Very strongly recommended.'
C. P. Snow, *Financial Times*

Theo Aronson, well known for his biographies
of the royal houses of Europe, is ideally
qualified to tell the story of the strange
partnership between the formidable Widow of
Windsor and the flamboyant Jew who once
wrote 'my nature demands that my life should
be perpetual love.'
But were they so ill-matched? Both needed the
intimate support of someone of the opposite
sex and each responded to the romanticism of
the other.
By the mid 1870s the personal and political
association between the imperialist Prime
Minister Disraeli and his Queen Empress was
in full flower. It was a relationship which
brought happiness and fulfilment to them
both.

'A sensitive and stylish account of their
relationship ... skilfully and sympathetically
described. Aronson has produced an
illuminating and entertaining book.'
Observer

0 304 31433 1

THE WORLD OF YESTERDAY
An Autobiography

Stefan Zweig, poet, dramatist, biographer
and novelist died by his own hand, exiled
in Brazil in 1942 'the world of my own
language having disappeared for me and
my spiritual home, Europe, having
destroyed itself.'
He left for publication a remarkable
autobiography: as a boy in Vienna he met
Brahms; he knew Freud, Hofmannsthal,
Richard Strauss and Rilke; he spent an
afternoon with Rodin and listened to
Yeats reading poetry in London. But as he
saw the effects of war and Hitler's rise to
power, politics took precedence over
literature and he went into exile.

**'Reminiscence is not Zweig's only claim
to attention. Looking back, in the midst
of world war for the second and more
terrible time, at the way he had come, he
wrote, he explained as Austrian, Jew,
author, humanist and pacifist all rolled
into one. It is this meditative strain which
is the making of his autobiography.'**
Times Literary Supplement

0 304 31436 6

EDMUND CAMPION

'Mr Waugh's study is a model of what a short
biography should be'.
Graham Greene

Evelyn Waugh presented his biography of
Edmund Campion, the Elizabethan poet,
scholar and gentleman who became the
haunted, trapped and murdered priest as 'a
simple, perfectly true story of heroism and
holiness.'
But it is written with a novelist's eye for the
telling incident and with all the elegance and
feeling of a master of English prose.
From the years of success as an Oxford scholar,
to entry into the newly founded Society of
Jesus and a professorship in Prague,
Campion's life was an inexorable progress
towards the doomed mission to England.
There followed pursuit, betrayal, a spirited
defence of loyalty to the Queen and a
horrifying traitor's death at Tyburn.

'Waugh's style is perfectly attuned to his
matter and the result is an experience of
indescribable poignancy for the imaginative
reader.'
Compton Mackenzie

0 304 31434 X